Judaism and Mysticism
According to Gershom Scholem

Scholars Press
Reprints and Translations Series

Published through the cooperation and support of the American Academy of Religion, the Society of Biblical Literature,
the American Society of Papyrologists, the American Philological Association, and Brown Judaic Studies.

JUDAISM AND MYSTICISM ACCORDING TO GERSHOM SCHOLEM
A Critical Analysis and Programmatic Discussion

by
Eliezer Schweid

Translated from the Hebrew,
with an Introduction
by
David Avraham Weiner

Literary Editor:
Caroline McCracken-Flesher

Scholars Press
Atlanta, Georgia

JUDAISM AND MYSTICISM
ACCORDING TO GERSHOM SCHOLEM
A Critical Analysis and Programmatic Discussion

by
Eliezer Schweid

Translated from the Hebrew, with an Introduction
by
David Avraham Weiner

© 1985
Scholars Press

The original Hebrew edition was published by
Magnes Press, The Hebrew University, Jerusalem,
as a title in the series, *Jerusalem Studies in Jewish
Thought*, Supplement II (1983). © 1983.

Library of Congress Cataloging in Publication Data

Schweid, Eliezer.
    Judaism and mysticism according to Gershom
Scholem.

    (Scholars Press reprints and translations series)
    Translation of : Mistitkah ve-Yahadut le-fi Gershom
Shalom.
    Includes index.
    1. Scholem, Gershom Gerhard, 1897 –   —Criticism and
interpretation. 2. Mysticism—Judaism—History. 3. Cabala—
History. I. McCraken-Flesher, Caroline.
II. Title. III. Series.
BM755.S295S3813   1985 296.7'1   85-8403
ISBN 0–89130–982–9
ISBN 0–89130–887–3 (alk. paper)

Printed in the United States of America
on acid-free paper

TABLE OF CONTENTS

TRANSLATOR'S FOREWORD TO THE ENGLISH EDITION OF ELIEZER SCHWEID'S *JUDAISM AND MYSTICISM ACCORDING TO GERSHOM SCHOLEM*

This volume initiates a long overdue discussion. It constitutes the first comprehensive and vigorous critique of Gershom Scholem's renowned work on Jewish mysticism. Eliezer Schweid, the author of this study, is a Professor of Jewish philosophy at the Hebrew University of Jerusalem. He is one of the most prominent Israeli scholars of Jewish thought. In the past, Schweid's published works have dealt primarily with Jewish philosophy, Hebrew literature, and Zionist ideology. The present volume is his effort to evaluate Gershom Scholem's views on mysticism and Jewish history.

Schweid begins his analysis by outlining the central assumptions behind Scholem's voluminous writings. He goes on to argue that Scholem's theoretical suppositions produce an inaccurate portrait of biblical-prophetic religion, institutional Judaism, Jewish philosophy, Jewish theology, and modern Judaic scholarship. To the extent that Schweid's criticisms are valid, his book calls into question some fundamental premises of Scholem's scholarly enterprise.[1]

The philosopher Martin Buber reportedly remarked, "all of us have students, some of us have even created schools, but only Gershom Scholem has created a whole academic discipline."[2] In his groundbreaking studies, Gershom Scholem carefully laid the foundations for scholarly research into Jewish mysticism. His detailed works outline diverse trends in the long history of kabbalistic thought. These pioneering works have distinguished Gershom Scholem as a seminal figure in Judaic scholarship. Moreover,

---

1 It should be noted at the outset that Schweid's critique concentrates exclusively on the "larger picture" emerging from Scholem's writings. At no point does he challenge Scholem on matters of historical or literary detail. Indeed, Schweid pays tribute to Scholem's masterful analysis of mystical texts such as the Zohar and the Lurianic Kabbalah. He also points out that many cryptic kabbalistic sources were first exposed to philological-historical examination in the works of Gershom Scholem.
2 See "Literatur und Kunst," 11 June, 1967, *Neue Zuricher Zeitung.*

1

his ideas have gradually gained influence in a variety of disciplines, ranging from comparative history of religions to literary criticism.

Precisely because of Scholem's impact on contemporary thinkers, Schweid sees an urgent need to scrutinize his basic theoretical suppositions. In Schweid's estimation, the lack of such evaluations has enabled Scholem's idiosyncratic biases to filter into various areas of contemporary academic deliberation. The present volume is therefore designed to benefit "[those who] are liable to err and to lose [their] way. They may be misled by hidden prejudices deriving from the particular circumstances that affected the development of Gershom Scholem's personality and from the cultural environment in which he was raised."[3]

Schweid suggests that Scholem's writings on Judaism and mysticism are guided by a set of presuppositions that he formed as a youth in Germany during the first decades of this century.[4] According to Schweid, the young Scholem rejected the two central trends of German Judaism in his day: halakhic orthodoxy and progressive liberalism. He regarded orthodox Judaism as an ossified institutional system that stifled religious creativity. The liberal forms of Judaism were dismissed as apologetic, excessively rational, or simply lacking in authentic religious expression. Scholem ultimately concluded that neither orthodoxy nor liberalism possessed the regenerating force that sustained the Jewish religion throughout the generations. He came to believe that the historical vitality of the Jewish religion was embedded in its subterranean tradition of gnostic-kabbalistic mysticism. In Schweid's opinion, this basic intuition serves as the cornerstone of Scholem's monumental intellectual enterprise.

In his scholarly writings, Scholem characterized mysticism as the last and most crucial of three stages in the dialectical development

3 See p. 168 of this volume.
4 For a thorough analysis of the young Scholem's intellectual development and its impact on his approach to Jewish mysticism, see David Biale, *Gershom Scholem: Kabbalah and Counter-History*, Cambridge, Harvard University Press, 1978. Biale draws attention to several points that are not taken up by Schweid, including Walter Benjamin's impact on Scholem and the counter-rational anarchistic strain underlying Scholem's scientific historiography.

of religion. Historical religions begin with an initial stage of innocence in which religious believers spontaneously experience the immediate presence of the deity. This is followed by a process of institutionalization that creates an alienating distance between the religious believer and God. Mysticism resolves this condition of religious alienation by developing a mode of consciousness through which the believer recovers the direct experience of divine presence.

Schweid claims that this outlook led Scholem to challenge the view of Jewish mysticism advanced by his predecessors. Previous Judaic scholars, especially those associated with *Wissenschaft des Judentums,* had generally maintained that mysticism was alien to the historical and theological essence of Judaism. Scholem, by contrast, insisted that various trends of mystical thought played a central role in the history of the Jewish religion. He suggested that gnostic-kabbalistic thought was Judaism's hidden regenerative resource throughout the ages, enabling believing Jews to overcome halakhic institutionalization's alienating force. Accordingly, in his scholarly writings, Scholem attempted to prove that gnostic and kabbalistic mysticism were central elements in Judaism from the days of the early rabbinic legislators up to the dawn of the modern era. Scholem also tried to trace threads of kabbalistic thought in modern movements such as Hassidism, Haskalah, and Zionism. More significantly, he indicated that authentic mystical creativity was needed to resolve the religious crisis produced by contemporary Judaism's confrontation with modernity.

In this book, Schweid argues that Scholem's approach to mysticism generates a misleading portrait of Judaism's history. He supports his argument with diverse examples drawn from the entire spectrum of Scholem's work. To begin with, he maintains that Scholem's theoretical scheme is incompatible with the findings of biblical research and fails to account for the authentic forms of religious experience that have been expressed in non-mystical forms of Judaism. In addition, Schweid claims that Scholem provided a biased characterization of medieval Jewish philosophy in general, and of the works of Saadya Gaon and Maimonides in particular.

Schweid also rejects Scholem's partially sympathetic treatment of Sabbatianism and its mystical leader, Sabbatai Sevi. Scholem suggested that the antinomian movement of Sabbatianism may be seen as an authentic development of Jewish mystical consciousness. Schweid, by contrast, insists that Sabbatianism was a dangerous and "pathological" distortion of Jewish religious thought. In fact, says Schweid, the fate of Sabbatianism illustrates the absurdity of Scholem's belief that kabbalistic religion was the central force ensuring Judaism's vitality throughout the ages. For the Sabbatian debacle indicates that when kabbalism moves from the esoteric periphery to the center of religious expression, believers take a perilous turn toward illusory salvation; Judaism begins to destroy itself from within.

The concluding sections of Schweid's analysis deal with Scholem's critical attitude toward modern Judaic scholarship and theology. Schweid defends many thinkers who were challenged by Scholem, including Hermann Cohen, Franz Rosenzweig, Martin Buber, and the founders of the *Wissenschaft des Judentums* movement. He insists that Scholem's critique of these scholars and theologians was largely inaccurate and unfair. Schweid also questions Scholem's opinions about the contemporary condition of the Jewish religion. In effect, says Schweid, Scholem's outlook generates only one option for the modern Jew: to engage in an empathetic study of mystical texts while waiting for the eruption of a new Jewish mysticism. Schweid dismisses this position because it stifles a great deal of creative effort while advocating a resolution irrelevant to modernity — one that threatens to damage the Jewish religion from within.

Through his critique of Scholem, Schweid reveals his own paradigm of Jewish history and theology. Indeed, Schweid frequently uses Scholem's theory as a foil for presenting his alternative perspective. He locates the essence of Judaism in a particular historical worldview, rather than in mysticism. That is, Schweid believes that the Jewish religion sustained its vitality and continuity throughout the generations because Jewish thinkers preserved a particular conception of the historical relation between God and the Jewish people. This fundamental outlook is referred to by Schweid as "the historical myth of the people of Israel." The myth is structured by the prophetic-biblical narrative that begins with the creation of the universe and culminates in the messianic redemption. The narrative interweaves the tales of the patriarchs, the sinaitic revelation, the construction and destruction of the two temples, and the return to Zion. According to Schweid, this story was gradually aligned to legislated norms of action endowed with the authoritative status of revealed *Torah*.

Schweid maintains that the mythic worldview and its complementary way of life, the *halakhah,* convey the following message: God stands in a direct moral relationship with the Jewish people; the people must obey their God by consciously adhering to the injunctions of *Torah;* God responds to the people's display of worldly obedience by providentially governing their historical fate.

In Schweid's opinion, the distinctive logic of this myth enabled Jews to establish halakhic institutions without inevitably producing the religious alienation described by Scholem. That is, the institutionalization of the Jewish religion did not necessarily generate the alienation depicted in Scholem's tripartite scheme. To begin with, the interaction between God and man had been defined in a manner that enabled the institutions of Jewish Law (*halakhah*) to serve as means toward the immediate experience of divine presence. Furthermore, even during crises of religious alienation, the time-honored mythic worldview was not necessarily conducive to a mystical religious consciousness. When Jews felt estranged from the deity, they traditionally assumed that God had concealed his face because the people had induced his wrath. Under these circumstances, says Schweid, the appropriate response was atonement, rather than kabbalistic-mystical creativity. That is, the Jew would not try to break into God's other-worldly chambers by means of a mystical technique. Rather, believers traditionally scrutinized their worldly actions and atoned for their moral and religious shortcomings. Accordingly, claims Schweid, prominent Jewish thinkers throughout the ages have stressed the worldly relationship between God and man, and the value of ethical behavior in the realm of "the here and now." In Schweid's estimation, the emphasis placed upon these elements has helped to ensure the vitality of the Jewish religion and the continuity of the Jewish people throughout the centuries.

Schweid's work may thus be understood as a twofold polemic. His primary aim is to debunk Scholem's notion that the life-blood of Judaism runs in its subterranean artery of gnostic-kabbalistic mysticism. Schweid believes that this conception inappropriately tilts the scales against several central themes in Jewish history and theology. The author's secondary goal is to reaffirm certain points of view that were explicitly challenged by Scholem. That is, he attempts to formulate a rejoinder on behalf of thinkers Scholem criticized. Schweid is particularly keen to defend the religious worldview proposed by medieval philosophers such as Maimonides, Saadya Gaon, and Bahey Ibn Pekudah. He insists that Scholem underestimated the importance of the rational and moral Judaism advanced by these thinkers. Schweid also seeks to reestablish the significance of the modern existentialist theologians Hermann Cohen, Franz Rosenzweig, and Martin Buber, for unlike Scholem, these thinkers tended to stress the prophetic-biblical matrix of Jewish religious consciousness. Moreover, they advocated the realization of divine presence in the earthly "here and now," and rejected the gnostic-kabbalistic urge to achieve divine experience by negating and transcending the world.

In short, this work highlights a conflict between two opposing paradigms of Jewish history and theology. On the one hand, Scholem upholds the kabbalistic tradition as the core of vital Jewish religion, the crucial subterranean stream preserving and nurturing Judaism throughout the generations. Schweid, on the other hand, sees the historical-biblical myth and its complementary institutions of *halakhah* as the source of Judaism's uncanny vitality. While he is willing to concede that kabbalistic mysticism served a valuable function in Jewish history as long as it was confined to esoteric circles, he suggests that scholars and theologians who move *kabbalah* from Judaism's periphery to its center distort the historical religion of the Jewish people.

One may argue that Schweid's adherence to his own paradigm produces an incomplete view of Jewish history and a rather harsh critique of Scholem's positions. Indeed, Schweid himself seems to recognize that his assessments are influenced by a personal preference for the rational, moral, institutional and national aspects of Judaism. Moreover, in order to advance his own theses, Schweid at times provides schematic interpretations of Scholem's complex and enigmatic ideas.[5] Nevertheless, this work marks an advance in the scholarly literature. To date, with very few exceptions, scholars have been reluctant to criticize the fundamental assumptions underlying Scholem's writings. This volume promises to initiate fruitful deliberations upon the basic views of Gershom Scholem, who undoubtedly will be remembered as one of our generation's greatest scholars.

My translation was guided by one basic objective, to render the author's Hebrew into clear and intelligible English prose. Thus, the English version often fails to reproduce the form of Schweid's sentences and paragraphs. I can only hope that the clarity of the content will compensate the reader for this loss of style. For the benefit of the English reader, I have also supplemented the text with a detailed Index and Table of Contents.

In conclusion, I would like to thank those who offered assistance at various stages of this project. First and foremost is my friend and teacher, Professor Jacob Neusner, who suggested this work to me and made important contributions at every juncture. Hillel Halkin offered instructive advice regarding the art of translation. My discussions with Rabbi James Ponet and Professors David Biale,

---

5 The philosopher Nathan Rotenstreich elaborates this criticism in the essay "Clarification of Concepts," in Hebrew, *Jerusalem Studies in Jewish Thought,* Vol. III, 3, 1983-4. In Rotenstreich's estimation Schweid does not do justice to Scholem's complex hermeneutical approach to religious texts.

Aviezer Ravitizky, Ivan Marcus, Maurice Natanson and Joshua Sherman helped me to appreciate some subtle issues addressed in this book. Professor Eliezer Schweid reviewed the translation and made many crucial suggestions. The Richter foundation supplied funds for this publication. Caroline McCracken-Flesher edited the translation and improved its quality significantly. I am also grateful to my dear friends, Eldar Shafir and Yossi Shain, for reading parts of the translation. My brother and sister-in-law, Daniel and Mindy Ivry, created a peaceful environment in the Galilean settlement of Yodephat, where most of this translation was completed. Finally, my beloved parents, Eugene and Anita Weiner, provided support and encouragement that were essential to the completion of this task.

Jerusalem-New Haven
March 1984

David Avraham Weiner

PREFACE

JUDAISM AND MYSTICISM ACCORDING TO GERSHOM SCHOLEM:

A Critical Analysis
and Programmatic Discussion

Eliezer Schweid

Gershom Scholem's writings consist primarily of scientific, philological-historical studies of the Jewish people's religious literature. The importance of Scholem's scholarly enterprise and its influence on Judaic studies are not at issue. Gershom Scholem rightly is considered one of the founders — indeed the greatest among the founders — of the scientific discipline that examines mysticism in general, and Jewish mystical movements in particular. He has influenced subsequent research through his scholarly findings, his methodology, and his views regarding Jewish mysticism, its essence, and its place in the Jewish people's history. Scholem's influence can be traced not only in his own field, but also in related areas of Judaica. Further, he has influenced scholars whose work transcends the range of Judaic studies, especially historians of Christianity. These facts alone call for a critical examination of Scholem's viewpoints and conclusions. Indeed such an examination seems necessary for ensuring the fruitful progress of scholarly research in all the above fields.

The unique status of Scholem's enterprise surpasses the boundaries of scholarship. Relatively speaking, he rarely expressed his own views on pressing matters concerning the Jewish religion and the Jewish people's fate. Nevertheless, his writings generated a resounding response and a keen interest among Jewish and non-Jewish thinkers whose interest in Judaism focused on contemporary concerns. The attention they paid to Scholem's words expressed their yearning for a message that transcended the "dry" historical data, and indeed, many of Scholem's readers seemed actually to find such a message in his books. Consequently, Gershom Scholem emerged as one of the monumental figures of Jewish thought in our day.

Let us emphasize, however, that we are dealing here with a problematic issue. A certain complexity and ambivalence surround both Scholem's explicit attitude to his scholarly enterprise and the means through which his work influenced others. Gershom Scholem himself tended strongly to emphasize his status as a philological and historical scholar: he was merely a "professor," not a philosopher, a theologian or a prophet.[6] He portrayed himself as a man whose vocation was to reveal minute details in a portrait of past events. But nevertheless, by periodically publishing impressive essays, Scholem justified and even intensified his readers' anticipation of a message with contemporary significance. These essays clearly were tied in with the results and conclusions of Scholem's historical studies, yet they seemed to transcend his scholarly work.[7] Scholem's audience granted him the status of an authoritative Jewish thinker. Why? To large extent because of his unique synthesis which interwove historical scholarship with a contemporary message. His scholarly research included a message, and thereby endowed that message with authority. Examples of this synthesis will emerge time and again throughout our analysis of Scholem's work, and will thus be examined extensively in the subsequent discussion. In any case, Scholem's unique fusion of past and present provides a further reason for carefully attending to a critical analysis of his conceptual system.

This volume thus examines Gershom Scholem's worldview. We are particularly interested in the conclusions suggested by his conceptions of Judaism and Jewish history as they pertain to contemporary issues of Jewish religion and nationalism. The definition of our goal presupposes a distinction between (a) the

6 See Gershom Scholem, *Major Trends in Jewish Mysticism,* New York, Shocken, 1946, p. 350 (D.W.).
7 These articles were gathered together in a special Hebrew volume entitled *Devarim Be'Go (Explications and Implications),* Tel-Aviv, 1975. This extensive collection deals with a wide spectrum of issues.

scholarly data accumulated through Scholem's bibliographical, philological and historiographical work, and (b) the conceptual network generated on the periphery of Scholem's scholarly findings. Obviously, the scholarly findings must also be subjected to exposition and examination. Gershom Scholem's students have addressed this task in the past, and presumably they will continue to do so in the future. Yet today we seem to face a special task that transcends the objectives of routine scholarship.

We have already noted several reasons for undertaking our project. Let us add yet another. Scholem was allotted an extraordinary degree of scientific authority because of his impressive achievements in a wide range of scholarly areas that previously had been explored by only a handful of scholars. This general approbation to a large extent curbed any critique of his programmatic views. From time to time, dissenting voices were heard and several of these voices were sharply critical (especially those deriving from semi-orthodox thinkers who were deeply distressed by Scholem's views on Sabbatianism).[8] But on the whole, the so-called academic world seems to have accepted most of Scholem's

8 The sharpest and most famous critique of Scholem was advanced by Professor Baruch Kurzweil. See "Notes on Gershom Scholem's Sabbatai Sevi" and "The Discomfort in History and Judaic Scholarship" in Kurzweil's book, *Ba-Ma'avak Al Arakhei Hayahadut,* in Hebrew, Jerusalem and Tel-Aviv, Shocken, 1969. Upon its publication, this book caused a great stir and initiated a public controversy in which some of the scholars of the Hebrew University participated.

views. Silence implied consent. In any case, there was no systematic response.[9]

Admittedly, the above distinction between (a) scientific findings, and (b) views generated on their periphery, is not a simple one. Such a distinction invites criticism. On the one hand, the findings themselves are surely tied in with Scholem's phenomenological and historiosophical generalizations. On the other hand, by preserving this distinction carefully, will we not find that our discussion is limited to a very small number of articles that Scholem distinguished from his larger scientific corpus and depicted as auxiliary works? This question is especially problematic. Scholem did not see fit to write a systematic summary of his own views as a Judaic scholar. Indeed, he exhibited remarkable restraint in this regard. His few short essays on his own systematic views seem like sporadic eruptions when compared to the overflowing stream of his scientific scholarship. As we noted above, Scholem usually sought to present himself to the reader in the image of an academic "professor," an expert on things past.

9 There were in fact several controversies over particular scholarly details. For instance a controversy was initiated by Professor Isaiah Tishby's critical essay on the issue of messianism in late Hassidism. See Isaiah Tishby, *Netivei Emmunah Uminnut,* in Hebrew, Jerusalem, Bialik Foundation, 1982; see also Professor Ismar Schorsh's objections to Scholem's critique of modern Judaic scholarship in "From Wolfenbittel to Wissenschaft des Judentums," *LB* 1422, 1977, pp. 109-28.

At this juncture, let us also refer the reader to the first monograph dealing with Gershom Scholem's conceptual and scholarly enterprise: David Biale's *Kabbalah and Counter-History,* Cambridge, Harvard University Press, 1979. Readers of Biale's book will find much information valuable for understanding Scholem's enterprise. The book focusses especially upon Scholem's cultural-historical background and the sources that helped crystallize Scholem's scholarly approach to Jewish mysticism. Biale also makes a serious, but ultimately unsuccessful effort to present Scholem's views as a full-fledged systematic outlook. Biale's book fails primarily because the author neither develops a critical approach to Scholem's views nor expresses an independent opinion, based on his own research, regarding the speculative and historical questions that concerned Scholem. In our opinion, it is very difficult properly to present Scholem's views and to penetrate the thicket of contrary assertions, ambiguities and dialectical tensions in Scholem's writings unless one has independent critical reflection. One cannot attain such reflection without first conducting independent research in the history of ancient and modern Jewish thought. If one reaches the issues discussed by Scholem solely through Scholem's studies themselves, one will almost automatically tend to justify Scholem's position and to explain away contradictions and ambiguities without penetrating their root causes. Indeed, this case is characteristic of the attitude adopted by Scholem's readers. The uniqueness of Scholem's expertise in his field ruled out almost any criticism whatsoever.

The message that nevertheless erupted from his scholarly writings was thus interwoven with the scientific data he collected. This surely does not facilitate the labor of those who attempt to summarize and critically reexamine Scholem's general outlook upon Judaism.

Yet our task is not impossible, and it does not presuppose an arbitrary separation between scientific data and general conceptions. Nor must we restrict ourselves to a small sample of articles peripheral to Scholem's major enterprise. A careful examination reveals that Scholem's writings can be classified into four different types. This classification is based upon the methodology employed in a given work, as well as the definition and scope of its topic.

I. Bibliographic and philological essays on a specific subject such as a particular literary source, an individual thinker, etc. . . . In such essays, Scholem's task is strictly scientific and professional. To this category belong scores of articles that appeared in scientific journals. These essays generally served as constituent parts of larger historiographical constructions.

II. Books dealing with a larger subject, such as a trend or trends in Jewish mysticism, or significant historical events relating to a mystical movement. To this category belong works such as *The Origins of the Kabbalah,*[10] *Major Trends in Jewish Mysticism,*[11] *and Sabbatai Sevi.*[12]

III. Essays devoted to phenomenological analysis of central motifs or categories in Jewish mysticism and theology. To this category belong some of the most influential essays written by Scholem, such as "Redemption Through Sin,"[13] and "The Messianic Idea in Judaism,"[14] "Revelation and Tradition as

10 Gershom Scholem, *The Origins of Kabbalah,* in Hebrew, Jerusalem and Tel-Aviv, Shocken, 1948.
11 Gershom Scholem, *Major Trends in Jewish Mysticism,* New York, Shocken, 1941.
12 Gershom Scholem, *Sabbatai Sevi: The Mystical Messiah,* trans. R.J. Werblowsky, Princeton University Press, 1973.
13 The English version of this essay was published in Gershom Scholem, *The Messianic Idea in Judaism,* New York, Shocken, 1972.
14 *Ibid.*

Religious Categories in Judaism,"[15] "Three Types of Jewish Piety,"[16] etc. . . . .

IV. Essays and articles dealing with contemporary issues. Three of these works are especially noteworthy: "Reflections on the Science of Judaism," "Reflections on Jewish Mysticism in Our Time," and "Reflections on Jewish Theology."[17]

In addition to these sources, one must also consider Scholem's autobiographical work, *From Berlin to Jerusalem*.[18] I may also draw upon another, more personal source: my encounters with Gershom Scholem in lectures, seminars, and discussion groups. In these contexts, one discovered the vital dialectical connection between Scholem's scholarly research and the emotional motivations and conceptual inspirations that influenced him.

Obviously, a significant body of scientific data is embedded in each of the last three categories enumerated above. Yet the analysis, organization and classification of the data express Scholem's idiosyncratic outlook — at times even explicitly. Through his own individual perspective, Scholem generates innovative analyses, interpretations, and generalizations, and he often arrives at bold and far-reaching conclusions. Consequently, anyone examining Scholem's scholarly writings will not find it difficult to distinguish between (a) professional exposition and clarification, and (b) idiosyncratic outlooks. The latter are designed to convey a portrait, attach specific meanings, or lead to certain conclusions. Indeed it is obvious that the message conveyed to Scholem's readers derives from these idiosyncratic outlooks which permeate all his writings. Therefore, our analysis need not focus on the margins of Scholem's literary enterprise. On the contrary, our discussion moves between

15 *Ibid.*
16 See *Ariel: Review of Arts and Letters in Israel,* No. II, 1973f.
17 See *Explications and Implications,* in Hebrew, pp. 71-83, 385-404, 557-590. The essay "Reflections on Jewish Theology" appears in English in *Jews and Judaism in Crisis,* New York, Shocken, 1976, pp. 261-297.
18 Gershom Scholem, *Mi-Berlin Le-Yerushalayim,* Tel-Aviv, Am-Oved, 1983. This text appears in abridged form in English; see *From Berlin to Jerusalem: Memories of My Youth,* trans. H. Zohn, New York, Shocken, 1960.

diverse strands of Scholem's work as if through a unified literary corpus.

We may now point out that Scholem collected a massive body of scholarly data which provides a solid foundation for his analysis and interpretation. But this material does not necessarily lead directly to Scholem's own views. The same data can be interpreted entirely differently when viewed in conjunction with the findings of other scholars dealing with Jewish mysticism and various relevant fields in theology, sociology of religion, and historiography. In fact, if one disregards Scholem's almost exclusive preoccupation with Jewish mysticism, one may use his data to substantiate an entirely different viewpoint. We will try to establish this claim subsequently. Yet to meet this challenge, we need not enter a detailed discussion of Scholem's bibliographical, philological, and historical findings themselves.

In accordance with our objectives, the following volume presents these three analytical and expository elements:

A. A brief summary of Scholem's views on mysticism, on Jewish mysticism's specific characteristics, and on its relation to other trends of the Jewish religion, as well as its role in the formation of the Jewish people's destiny.
B. A critical examination of Scholem's views on the above issues. This examination will assess Scholem's treatment of various mystical trends throughout the major periods of Jewish history.
C. A proposal for an alternative to Scholem's programmatic approach.

The first task will be taken up separately at the outset, while the two remaining concerns will be addressed intermittently throughout the remainder of the volume. The discussion will be structured as follows. First, we will explore the problem of defining mysticism in general and of characterizing Jewish mysticism in particular. The subsequent sections deal with the approach to mysticism in Judaism's literary sources throughout the generations. This discussion will be presented in chronological order. The final part of our analysis assesses the weight and contribution of Jewish mysticism in the history of Jewish thought. That is, we will compare the role of mysticism to that of other trends in modern Jewish religious thought.

Some readers may be surprised by the structure of our discussion. Let me therefore provide a few brief explanatory comments. First, a structure composed of a summary followed by a more detailed critical analysis may at times generate redundancies. In the critical section, the reader will encounter points that were already mentioned in the earlier section. Such repetition is normally regarded as a stylistic flaw. But sometimes such redundancy has a justification that overrides the concern for structural clarity. If Gershom Scholem himself had summarized his views in a special philosophical essay, it would be methodologically unnecessary to provide a "dogmatic" exposition of his views at the outset of this volume. But Scholem refrained from offering such a systematic and comprehensive exposition of his views. Furthermore, his mode of expression in various essays generates, as we shall see, many difficulties and ambiguities. Consequently, it is methodologically necessary to begin with a brief and synoptic exposition of Scholem's major theses and to point to the difficulties inherent in formulating a clear definition of his principal ideas. Only after presenting a model which the reader can keep in view may we advance a systematic critical analysis that both outlines Scholem's opinions in detail and examines them in depth. The methodological advantage of this type of structure will hopefully compensate the reader for the cumbersome repetition of several ideas.

Secondly, some readers will surely be surprised by my effort to present my own outlook in conjunction with a critique of Gershom Scholem's views. Does this not illegitimately exploit a discussion of the views of a famous scholar in order to substantiate the critic's alternative views? Indeed, there is such an exploitation in the following volume. Yet, in my view, this maneuver is not illegitimate. On the contrary, this is how it should be. One can, of course, offer criticism without providing a formulated alternative. But obviously, some alternative perspective is always embedded at the foundation of a systematic critique. It is preferable to expound one's argument fully and directly. Moreover, we are dealing with a programmatic controversy, and in such arguments one is required to take a stand and to offer an alternative view to that which one attempts to undermine. In any case, this is my expressed orientation.

Finally, some readers surely will object to my method of interweaving and synthesizing a critical discussion together with the exposition of my alternative outlook. It would, of course, have been possible to separate these two endeavors and to devote a separate chapter to each. Yet I preferred a unified discussion because the various conceptual issues are all woven of a single fabric. The considerations that led to the critique are identical with those lying at the foundation of my alternative viewpoint. But admittedly this may be the result of my own personal way of thinking. In concluding these introductory comments, it is appropriate to reveal that the following volume summarizes the long formative journey of a student struggling with the teaching of his master. My personal, subjective experience may thus have dictated the discussion's structure and style. But I share this predicament with most of those presently studying the Jewish religion and struggling with its contemporary problems. We are all to some measure or in some way the students of Gershom Scholem, and we must first confront his monumental enterprise before setting out to develop our own approaches.

Through this last sentence, I convey the wish that this critique will not be understood as an effort to undermine Scholem's legacy and to burn the bridges between his generation and ours. Rather, my work is designed to arouse a discussion that is a prerequisite for renewal and continuity.

PART I.
SYNOPTIC EXPOSITION

CHAPTER 1

RECONSTRUCTING SCHOLEM'S VIEWS

i. Defining Mysticism

Gershom Scholem's views regarding modern Judaic scholarship, the Jewish religion, and the place of mysticism in Jewish history are far less clear and definitive than his sharp and lucid style suggests. A survey of essays which Scholem wrote at different times reveals not only that his emphases vary, but also that some of his statements are equivocal or even contradictory. Yet the overall orientation of his work is perfectly clear. In Scholem's view, mysticism constitutes Judaism's substantive essence while all other elements are merely receptacles or accoutrements. This orientation is attested to by the simple fact that Scholem's vast scholarly enterprise is devoted entirely to Jewish mysticism, from its beginnings during the days of the second Temple, up to its latest transformation in modern times. Scholem also persistently refrained from thoroughly examining other areas of the Jewish religion. We thus have both positive and negative evidence that he regarded mysticism as the source from which the Jewish religion regenerates itself. Although the orientation of Scholem's research may be clear, it is far from obvious that this orientation is intellectually justified. Indeed, it seems that at times, Scholem himself was not entirely sure that his judgement was correct; his prose is sufficiently ambiguous to allow for an alternative assessment of the place of non-mystic religion within Judaism.

We can discern this lack of clarity even in Scholem's first attempts to define the term 'mysticism,' especially in his efforts to explain how this term applies to diverse religious movements within Judaism. The definitions which he proposes in several different articles are neither identical nor consistent in emphasis.[19]

19 The various definitions of mysticism are discussed in the following essays:
    a. *Major Trends in Jewish Mysticism* (New York: Shocken Books, 1941), first lecture.

In one interesting example he advances a definition which actually undermines the idea that authentic mysticism can exist within Judaism's development.[20] Scholem prefers to let this definition remain unquestioned, sealed within its context. But to be consistent on the larger scale, Scholem had to "revise" definitions that were generally accepted by scholars of Christian and Islamic mysticism. We can nonetheless appreciate why he sometimes contented himself with a definition so inclusive and vague that it seems questionable whether mysticism can be distinguished from other types of experiential religious practice.[21]

b. "Reflections on the Possibility of Jewish Mysticism in Our Day," in *Explications and Implications: Writings on Jewish Heritage and Renaissance,* in Hebrew (Tel-Aviv: Am Oved, 1975), pp. 71-83.

c. "Jewish Esoterica and the Kabbalah," *Explications and Implications,* pp. 230-269.

d. "The Concept of Redemption in *Kabbalah,*" *Explications and Implications,* pp. 191-216.

Scholem also found it necessary to clarify this issue further in several of his other essays, especially in those collected in the volume *On the Kabbalah and Its Symbolism,* trans. Ralph Manheim (New York: Shocken Books, 1965).

20 When I speak here of mysticism, I may legitimately be asked to what I refer. And indeed, I hesitate to burden you with definitions, for no one really knows what mysticism is except the mystics themselves, and they have different opinions that vary in accord with their particular subjective understanding. There are as many definitions as there are writers on this subject. Nevertheless, one cannot avoid this issue entirely. To begin with, I will say that if we refer to mysticism as the direct, unmediated unification with God, then Jewish mysticism does not exist at all. Within the framework of Jewish tradition, there is no such thing, for such unification represents a boldness that was seen as impossible in the traditional terms of all those who belong in the category of "Israel." But if we define mysticism as an awareness or an experiential perception of divine matters, then Jewish mysticism certainly exists in diverse and multi-faceted forms. It has existed for two thousand years, since the days of the masters of *Merkavah,* and since the days of the exceptional mystic named Paulus Mathersus, up to the present day . . .

Explications and Implications, p. 72.

21 This is actually the same definition proposed in the article "Reflections on the Possibility of Jewish Mysticism in Our Day," where Scholem writes, "But if we define mysticism as an experiential consciousness or sensation of divine matters, then Jewish mysticism certainly exists in many forms and in a multitude of shades." But even the definition set forth at the outset of the essay "Jewish Esoterica and the *Kabbalah*" is inclusive and vague: "By the name 'Hebrew mysticism' or *Kabbalah* in the wide sense, we designate the totality of trends in Judaism that strive to reach a religious consciousness beyond the mind's capacity, and that can be attained by delving into the depths of one's self through contemplation and the inner illumination deriving from contemplation." It is doubtful that this definition helps us to distinguish between mysticism and religious philosophy. It is also doubtful that this definition points to the distinctness of classical *Kabbalah* as an experience emerging from contemplation of the *Torah.*

The most extensive discussion of this problem appears in the first chapter of the classic book, *Major Trends in Jewish Mysticism*. We assume that, in this chapter, Gershom Scholem expressed his point of view in its most complete and authoritative form. We may thus posit the definition proposed there as a base from which to discuss his theory of mysticism and mysticism's place in Judaism. It is worth noting, however, that Scholem apparently was less confident in his definition and in the conclusions it implies than the limited context of his chapter would suggest. Throughout the subsequent discussion we will notice substantive consequences of Scholem's ultimate uncertainty.

For an obvious methodological reason, Scholem needed thoroughly to examine the concept "mysticism" in his book's first chapter. He had to define the topic of his lectures and to justify his application of the term 'mysticism' to a wide spectrum of diverse religious movements within Judaism. At the same time, he had to confront the view accepted by many modern scholars and philosophers of Judaism that mysticism is a negative religious phenomenon essentially alien to Judaism. The theory goes thus: since mysticism is alien, attempts to graft any part of it onto classical Judaic sources never succeeded; such failed attempts drew corruptions and pathological distortions in their wake.[22] In opposition, Scholem wished to demonstrate that Jewish mysticism does indeed exist and that mysticism is not only a positive form of religious creativity but also a necessary manifestation of religious expression itself. Scholem also hoped to show that mysticism was the very source through which Judaism renewed itself from one generation to the next. To accomplish this objective, Scholem

22 This issue forms part of the polemic conducted by Scholem against the scholarship of *Wissenschaft des Judentums* which antedated his own work, particularly his critique of Graetz. We will subsequently provide an overall discussion of this polemic, but it is worth noting that Scholem saw fit to mention this criticism in the first lecture of his book *Major Trends in Jewish Mysticism*. As Scholem says, "The Great Jewish scholars of the past century whose conception of Jewish history is still dominant in our days, men like Graetz, Zunz, Geiger, Luzzatto and Steinscheider, had little sympathy — to put it mildly — for the *Kabbalah*. At once strange and repellent, it epitomized everything that was opposed to their own ideas and to the outlook which they hoped to make predominant in modern Judaism" (p. 1).

found it necessary to suggest his own definition of mysticism at the outset. He also had to demonstrate how this definition applies to the Jewish religion and to explain how Jewish mysticism can be distinguished from other manifestations of mystical religiosity.

From the very first step, however, one senses a problem behind Scholem's analysis. Before he did anything else, Scholem had to reject two definitions of the mystical phenomenon that were commonly adopted by scholars of comparative religious studies.[23] One of these seemed too broad to him, the other too narrow.

The broad definition designates mysticism as any experiential religion that is concerned with man's immediate experience of a divine presence. In response, Scholem argues that not every immediate experience of divine presence is mystical. Only a certain specifiable subset of these experiences is truly mystical.

From the wide spectrum of mystical movements within various religions, the narrow definition accepts only those characteristics which can be conjoined to form 'pure mysticism.' According to this second definition, the human soul experiences mysticism when it identifies itself with a divinity to the point of eliminating its own separate existence and merging with the divine infinitude.

If one accepts the first definition, there is no difficulty in applying the concept of mysticism to the Jewish religion. But such an application designates no distinctly meaningful content that can advance our understanding of the subject-matter at hand. Almost any religious expression will fall within the category of mysticism as long as it does not consist merely of a mechanical observance of injunctions. As for the second definition, it leads to the unacceptable conclusion that mysticism exists only in pagan religions or in religions with a clear pagan motif.

Scholem draws nearer to his own preferred definition when he challenges the tendency to extract a single element of 'pure mysticism' from manifestations of diverse institutional religions. Mysti-

---

23 Scholem deals especially with two works that he held in high regard:
 a. Rufus Jones, *Studies in Mystical Religion* (London: n.p., 1909).
 b. Evelyn Underhill, *Mysticism* (London: n.p., 1926).

cism, so he claims, is not a single general phenomenon. There are many mysticisms in the world and each is tied in with one of the institutional religions. More generally, he argues that each religion develops its own mysticism and this offshoot is nurtured and distinguished by the sources of the particular institutional religion within which it developed. There are pagan mysticisms, there is Christian mysticism, and there is Islamic mysticism. These mysticisms possess characteristics which are distinctive of Paganism, Christianity, and Islam respectively. Jewish mysticism exists along these same lines. Each form of mysticism must be studied in its own right, rather than by comparison to some ideal model. Consequently, even if there are substantial differences between Jewish mysticism and the mysticism found in other religions, it still does not follow that no mysticism is possible within Judaism. At the same time, the concept of mysticism should not be regarded merely as a vague common denominator. There is a specific feature shared by mystical phenomena of various religions. This common feature finds expression in the distinction between the mystical and institutionalized elements of these religions. We thus arrive at the following definition: mysticism is a particular stage — and in Scholem's opinion a necessary stage — in the evolution of any religion. Each religion passes through this stage in accord with its distinctive characteristics and cultural-historical circumstances.

Such a definition presupposes that religions evolve in a particular way. According to Scholem's scheme, every religion passes through three stages (and it seems that a religion can pass through the sequence several times during its history). First arises the stage of innocent religion. During this stage, the myth generated expresses the direct, spontaneous experience of the religious believer. Perhaps this myth is best understood as that which organizes daily experience so directly, man has no sense of a partition between himself and the Gods revealed to him. The myth is experienced spontaneously and with certainty. Second comes the stage of institutionalized religion. Here the spontaneity is curbed, modes of worship are defined, and specific hierarchies

25

are determined. The myth no longer organizes the believing person's immediate experience of reality. Furthermore, the believer can no longer appeal directly to his god. This inevitably creates a sense of alienation. Last is the mystical stage. Here, people who yearn for the immediate experience of divine presence search for a way to overcome the bifurcation created by institutional religion. They strive to revert to the first stage, but it is clear that they cannot regain the necessary state of spontaneity. The experience of innocence has been enveloped. There is no longer an immediate identity between the myth and the manner in which man perceives the reality surrounding his everyday experience. The believer must crack the shell enveloping the hidden interiority, so reflexivity may replace spontaneity. The believer must scrutinize either the depths of his own existence or the depths of his environment. He needs to interpret everything anew and to uncover apertures through which he can glimpse or penetrate the desired region. Obviously, the simple myth no longer suffices for this purpose. What is required, in addition to the myth, is an "ideology" to explain the discrepancies between (a) man's immediate experience within his environment, and (b) the truth that is embedded in the myth. This is the task of theology, a vital component of mystical religion. Moreover, in order to pass from ordinary, alienated experience to experience within the sphere of concealed reality, mysticism needs to employ new means: symbols, rituals, and techniques for penetration, ascent, and discovery. Mysticism, therefore, is defined as experiential, reflexive religion. This faith can decipher enigmas and transport the believer from the sphere of mundane experience by means of a distinctive religious "technique." In Scholem's opinion, this definition of mysticism is quite applicable to Judaism. For although Judaism may have evolved in its own distinctive way, it necessarily passed through the same three stages as other religions.

At this juncture, however, we encounter a certain lack of clarity in Scholem's exposition. We are not offered a detailed description of the first two stages in his tripartite scheme. Thus, we know neither when the stage of spontaneous religion took place, nor the characteristics of this stage. Also, we are not informed about the institutionalization processes and their characteristics. It is nonetheless clear that, according to Scholem, mystical movements were already active in Judaism at the outset of the Tannaitic period, and since that time, there has been an unbroken chain of Jewish mysticism.

ii. Characteristics of Jewish Mysticism

Since each form of mysticism draws its distinctive characteristics from the institutional religion within which it is generated, we must ask what Jewish mysticism drew from institutionalized Jewish religion.[24] Scholem notes that Jewish mysticism affirmed the authoritative position of both the holy scriptures, i.e., the *Torah*, the *Nevi'im* (Prophets), and the *Ketuvim* (Writings), and the books of Oral *Torah*. In other words, Jewish mysticism maintained the authority of tradition as a central religious category in Judaism.[25] The authority of revelation is thereby extended throughout the Jewish tradition. During the middle ages, the term *Kabbalah* came to designate Jewish mysticism. This concept affirms both the revealed authority of the Jewish sources and, at the same time, the institutional character of Jewish mysticism. The *Kabbala* (tradition) designates a true teaching that originates in prophetic revelation and is transmitted from one generation to the next by authorized and worthy *Mekubalim* (bearers of tradition).

By adopting the name *Kabbalah* Jewish mysticism cast itself in the image of Oral *Torah* — even in the image of directly inspired prophecy. Indeed, precisely for this reason, Jewish mysticism could afford to sustain the paradox that is the secret of religious renewal. This paradox consists in an extremely conservative loyalty to the

24 The following discussion is based on the first chapter of *Major Trends*.But Scholem repeated these characterizations in the essay "Jewish Esoterica and the *Kabbalah*."
25 This subject is especially developed in the extremely important essay "Revelation and Tradition as Categories in Judaism," in *The Messianic Idea in Judaism* (New York: Shocken Books, 1971). Scholem returned to this subject in the later comprehensive essay, "Reflections on Jewish Theology." In Scholem's view, this is actually one of the distinct characteristics of Judaism in general.

sources' authority coupled with courageous innovation and a semi-revolutionary approach to religious experience, theological viewpoints, and norms of religious behavior. This twofold approach prevents even a total reversal in the significance of central symbols and theological truths from disrupting the institutional religion's continuity. The authoritative stance of the institutional religion is not compromised. All innovation can be portrayed as merely the decipherment of hidden meanings buried in ancient sources.

According to Scholem this affirmation that Jewish sources were authoritative also determined Jewish mysticism's second distinguishing characteristic. Within the institutional Jewish religion, *Torah* occupies a central position. *Torah* is regarded as the word of God passed on to Israel's people. In Jewish mysticism, *Torah*'s status is sustained. *Torah* is mythically perceived as either an organic entity or a living figure standing between God and the people of Israel, linking them to one another.

Mysticism, claims Scholem, is based on a sensation of infinite distance between the divinity and the material universe, which includes man. Yet mysticism recognizes the divinity as the source of all that exists. This twofold belief generates alienation after the institutionalization of innocent religion. The problem then is as follows: how can man, who is corporeal, limited, and immersed in his own sins, rise up and return to his original existence within the sphere of divine spirituality? Mysticism needs mediators to connect finite man with a divinity concealed in infinitude.

In Jewish mysticism, the *Torah*, as a mystical entity, fulfills this mediating function. The *Torah* is divinity in its appeal to the world and to man.[26] That is to say, through the *Torah*, the infinite and anonymous divinity takes on a personality that can be addressed either by one name or by many names, each of which indicates a different aspect of the personal relation between God and man. It follows that *Torah*'s inner mystical essence is nothing other than

26 Scholem discusses this issue more extensively in the essay "The Meaning of the *Torah* in Jewish Mysticism" in *On the Kabbalah and Its Symbolism*.

28

the divinity's names in totality. Each name expresses one of the infinite divinity's personal relations to the universe. In this sense, the *Torah* is also the vehicle through which the world is created and governed. It is then obvious why the *Torah*, in its manifest form, is essentially a guide teaching Israelites the right way to approach God in thought and deed. By studying *Torah* in a manner that proceeds from the manifest external layer to the deeper, hidden interior, and by fulfilling the commandments with the kind of intention that links the physical deed with its spiritual significance, the believer will be transferred from exteriority to interiority. The believer thus becomes linked to the highest spheres of reality; he unites the lower and higher worlds. It is essential to recall that, in Jewish mysticism, it is the *Torah* that serves as the uniting element.

Torah's centrality dictates yet another of Jewish mysticism's characteristics, its adherence to linguistic symbolism as the primary symbolism in religious life. God created the world through speech. The *Torah*, as the instrument of creation and supervision, constitutes the totality of God's word. Thus, in a wider sense, the created universe is itself the word of God as well as the expression of his will and his wisdom. We find, therefore, that speech is the essence of the relationship between the hidden infinite divinity and the created reality. Within speech one can discern layer of meaning within layer of meaning; layer upon layer can be penetrated until speech attains to meaningful silence.

We said that the *Torah* constitutes the totality of God's names. Each name is a literal symbol with many meanings. Each letter within each name, on the one hand, and each arrangement of names, on the other, is regarded as a symbol with many meanings. The mystic's concern is to decipher the innumerable meanings of these literal symbols. By uncovering them, and by responding to them consciously and emotionally, the mystic becomes one with the *Torah*. As he becomes united with the *Torah*, the mystic is drawn upward and nearer to his God. Moreover, Jewish mysticism's "technique" for penetrating the layers that separate the manifest from the hidden is a procedure for deciphering the symbolism of *Torah*'s words. This technique simultaneously affirms and reinterprets another Jewish-Toraitic value, the notion that studying *Torah* for its own sake (lit. "for its own name") fulfills a divine injunction equivalent in its importance to all other injunctions combined.

Scholem designates a fourth characteristic unique to Jewish mysticism, the commitment to *halakhah*. This is Jewish mysticism's most "official" commitment to institutional Jewish religion. It is worth stressing, however, that here we have a dialectical relationship between institutionalized religion and mysticism. This relationship derives "necessarily" from what Scholem sees as mysticism's essentially ambivalent position vis-a-vis institutional religion. Mysticism needs institutional religion, but rebels against its alienated aspect. Thus, Jewish mysticism manifests an essentially ambivalent attitude to *halakhah* as the embodiment of institutional religion. For this reason, Scholem closely examines Jewish mysticism's antinomian tendencies.[27] He is especially attentive to these tendencies in his scholarly studies devoted to later *Kabbalah*, from the fourteenth century through Sabbatianism and its various transformations.

Sabbatianism is, of course, the ultimate expression of the antinomian tendency in mysticism. Yet it is impossible to understand why Scholem attributes Sabbatianism an important role in the history of Judaism unless one recognizes the basic postulate that antinomian Sabbatianism represents an essential expression of Jewish mysticism; indeed, Scholem suggests that Sabbatianism may contain the roots of that inventive motivation which enables mysticism to sustain Judaism from one generation to the next and to prevent its petrification.

---

27 For a substantiation of these assertions, see the following essays:
    a. "Toward an Understanding of the Messianic Idea in Judaism" in *The Messianic Idea*.
    b. "The Crisis of Tradition in Jewish Mysticism" in *On the Kabbalah*.
Also relevant to this are the early essays "Redemption Through Sin" and the larger work *Sabbatai Sevi: The Mystical Messiah*, trans. R.J. Werblowsky (Princeton: Princeton University Press, 1973).

Consequently, we may add the following to our assessment of Scholem: the antinomian motif in Jewish mysticism was one of the major factors attracting Scholem to the *Kabbalah*. Scholem's marked responsiveness to mysticism's antinomianism, and his special devotion to studying Sabbatianism and its transformations in the modern age, express an essential aspect of his relation to Judaism's historical predicament in his own day. Perhaps he found in Kabbalistic antinomianism an internal echo, or even an internal affirmation, of the modern Jew's rebellion against diasporic Judaism, particularly against the ghetto-characteristic of clinging to a severe halakhic stance. This characteristic constricts the creative and spiritual freedom of the individual Jew. And perhaps we may also assert that in Scholem's relation to Jewish scholarship and philosophy of his day, there was an echo of the same antinomian impulse that finds expression in the vital, religious spontaneity of the mystic. When rabbinic orthodoxy on the one hand and liberal rationalism on the other both claimed to be maintaining Judaism as an institution, Scholem protested against them both by appealing to the freedom inscribed upon the tablets of the law. He claimed that, in fact, it is antinomian mysticism that presently bears the secret of Judaism's vitality and continuity.[28]

---

28 It must be emphasized that this constitutes an effort to deduce conclusions from what is only alluded to in Scholem's formulations. In the aforementioned essays, and also in the essay "Redemption Through Sin," Scholem constructs a comparison with the modern idea of return to Zion. But he does not elaborate on this point. We find a slightly more detailed statement in the essay "Toward an Understanding of the Messianic Idea in Judaism." Of primary importance for our concerns is the distinction proposed between three types of forces acting within Talmudic Judaism: conservative, restorative and utopian. The *halakhah* is, of course, characterized as a conservative force, the force that maintained Judaism in the diaspora. Mysticism is classified among the restorative and utopian forces. Thus, there is an intense tension between these forces and the *halakhah*. But toward the conclusion of the essay, Scholem notes the heavy price that the people of Israel payed for the utopian messianism in mysticism. He says, "Little wonder that overtones of messianism have accompanied the modern Jewish readiness for irrevocable action in the concrete realm, when it set out on the utopian return to Zion." But in his opinion, Zionism "has not given itself up totally to messianism," and there remains an open question as to whether Zionists will prevail in the confrontation with the pulsating messianic-utopian element it contains. (See *The Messianic Idea*, pp. 35-6.) Statements in this same spirit were made by Scholem in a published interview. See *On Jews and Judaism in Crisis* (New York: Shocken Books, 1976), pp. 33-7. The same difficulty arises in Scholem's writings in "Reflections on the Possibility of Jewish Mysticism in our Day." In this context, the restrained and inferred

31

Nonetheless, throughout his scholarly studies, Scholem also saw fit to emphasize the opposite pole of this dialectical relationship between mysticism and institutionalized religion. Among the principal characteristics of distinctively Jewish mysticism, he lists the willingness to accept *halakhah's* yoke, not only in abiding by its accepted legislative verdicts, but also in admitting its distinctive discipline. Yet Kabbalists do not apply their method of scriptural interpretation to the realm of *halakhah*. Halakhic deliberation is a non-mystical discipline; mystical creativity in the area of *halakhah* manifests itself in clarifications of the rationale underlying the divine commandments (*mitzvot*).[29] Indeed, among the advantages of Jewish mysticism over Jewish philosophy, Scholem includes mysticism's success in endowing the ordinances with vital, symbolic significance. Mysticism transforms the willingness to accept the severely imposed yoke of formal ordinances into an expression symbolizing the spontaneity and sense of closeness of a living God. As long as Jewish mysticism succeeds in restraining its antinomian impulses and in existing within the circle of institutionalized religion, it is able to revive the *halakhah* by transforming its content while preserving its form.

This applies primarily to ritualistic *halakhah*, and more specifically to the established patterns of standard prayer. Obviously, crises relating to the sense of God's presence and proximity will initially find expression in the waning strength of institutionalized prayer. This liturgy ceases to offer the praying person an experience of his presence before God. The effort to overcome such a crisis

proximity to Sabbatianism can be sensed more intensely. Referring to the fundamental belief in *"Torah* from heaven," Scholem writes, "Whoever will not, or cannot, accept this matter becomes, objectively speaking, an anarchist. Today we are all, to a great extent, anarchists with respect to religion, and it is worth saying so openly . . . consequently, if we inquire the incursion of mystical stimuli in Judaism today, we find ourselves facing an actual reality of religious-Jewish anarchism" (*Explications and Implications*, pp. 80-81). Similar remarks are repeated by Scholem in the essay "Who Is a Jew" (*Explications and Implications*, pp. 591-598). The question discussed in all these sources is how Judaism can persevere after the structures of *halakhah* have been breached. There is a great deal of skepticism in Scholem's words. In any case, against this background, it is natural for Sabbatianism to be perceived in modern movements in Judaism.

29 See primarily the first chapter of the book *Major Trends*.

must therefore be expressed in the search for a new way of praying, or in the discovery of new meanings in the existing prayers. Just as Jewish mysticism succeeded in renewing the tradition of studying *Torah*, by discovering a new layer of meaning, it also succeeded in rejuvenating established prayer. Through a daring, symbolic conceptualization of the liturgy's routine forms, Jewish mysticism deciphered the enigmatic depths of prayer and discovered new significance in the general concepts of intention (*kavvanah*) and adherence (*devekut*).

Finally, Scholem notes that the Jewish religion's narrative-historical motifs serve an important function in Jewish mysticism. The motifs include the chosenness of the people of Israel, divine leadership in the history of the people of Israel, and the tripartite elements of destruction, exile, and redemption. These motifs penetrated and shaped the foundational myth of all Jewish mysticism. The historical themes took on new, daring, revolutionary significance. Nevertheless, there was also a clear line of continuity.

iii. The Role of Mysticism in Jewish History

As we noted, Scholem designed his definition of mysticism and his characterization of a specifically Jewish form of mysticism to substantiate the "thesis" he presented against the opinion which seemed to prevail among Judaic scholars before his time. Scholem's thesis was that the very same Jewish mysticism ignored in the scholarly literature actually embodied the secret of Judaism's essence and its capacity to renew itself from one generation to the next. It follows that by ignoring mysticism, one presents a Judaism emptied of its inner past. Furthermore, one clogs up the fruitful streams which should nourish Judaism's future renewals.

This view, of course, presupposes that Jewish mysticism is an ancient and pristine expression of Judaism. We must emphasize that Scholem did not initially derive his supposition from historical research. Rather, it was an a priori premise with which he embarked upon his scholarly work. At that time, the facts which

Scholem later revealed were not even partially known. His initial premise was an intuitive insight derived from empathetic observation of Jewish mysticism. When the mystical literature was revealed to Scholem from behind the veil of the great modern Judaic scholars' rationalistic research, he sensed that he had touched Judaism's source. The source is primal, and the primal is, by definition, ancient. It clearly follows that by stubbornly unravelling the layers of historical testimony, one will discover the mystical artery at the ancient historical juncture where innocent Jewish religion first underwent a crisis of institutional alienation. This conclusion inaugurated a very long series of studies that reflect Scholem's struggle to find a scientific, historical-philological confirmation for his initial premise.[30]

For Scholem, this initial premise was more than a hypothesis. It was almost a central article of faith. Quite typical, in this regard, is the story Scholem would repeat enthusiastically in his lectures on the history of *Kabbalah*. The story relates Scholem's various discoveries during his research on the Book of *Zohar*'s origins. When was this book written? Where was it written? Who was the author? These questions were already the subject of controversy among the sages when the book first appeared in the thirteenth century. Controversy sharply separated the adherents of *Kabbalah* from its opponents. A scholar studying the history of *Kabbalah* will naturally strive to reach a clear position regarding such questions since they pertain to the central classic composition of Jewish mysticism. At the outset of his scholarly career, Scholem was guided by the intuition that the book of *Zohar* was indeed ancient, or at least consisted primarily of ancient traditions. But alas, to his great disappointment, he instead managed to substantiate a thesis which all the *Zohar*'s critical opponents had never succeeded in definitively establishing. He proved that the book of *Zohar* was

---

30 See especially Scholem's *Jewish Gnosticism, Merkabah Mysticism, and Talmudic Tradition* (New York: n.p., 1960).

written in Spain at the end of the thirteenth century by the Kabbalist, R. Moshe De Leon.[31]

This finding, however, did not lead Scholem to forsake his objective. Since the *Zohar* did not provide support for his desideratum, he saw fit to examine the most ancient literary documents available. In an effort to uncover the ancient mystical artery, he considered the literature of *Hekhalot* and *Shiur Komah*, as well as the external literature, and even the Tannaitic and Talmudic sources. In these studies, Scholem endeavored to substantiate three premises:

a. This literature is indeed very ancient, far more so than assumed by most of the solid scholars in Scholem's day. In other words, this literature contains evidence of a mystical tradition that can be traced to a point of origin as close as possible to the dawn of the second Temple period.

b. This literature expresses the beliefs and experiences of central personalities and leading parties in the Jewish people, not those of insignificant and marginal sects.

c. This literature is not solely the product of external influences. Even if such influences were absorbed, the literature remains, in its essence, the product of an original internal development within the Jewish religion. In other words, we have before us an artery of monotheistic mysticism.

It is true that Scholem subjected these premises to severe scientific examination. Moreover, he never claimed to prove more than he could deduce clearly and convincingly from the documents he managed to uncover and interpret.[32] Nonetheless, it is clear that we are dealing with conclusions that follow from Scholem's fundamental insight into the essence of mysticism and from the historical-philosophical theory he based upon this insight. If it is correct

31 See *Major Trends*, Ch. V.
32 And in truth, even after these studies, the question as to whether Jewish mysticism is an original development or a result of external influence remained in the category of issues requiring further study. A decisive answer to this question was not provided, nor is it likely that such an answer will be given in the future, in spite of the trend of recent studies, which will be mentioned in the subsequent pages.

to suppose that (a) mysticism is an inevitable response to the institutionalization and breakdown of innocent religion, and if indeed (b) halakhic religion should be seen as the institutionalizing phase of innocent Jewish religion, and if (c) the diverse currents and sects in Israel during the days of the second Temple are expressions of the struggle with the historical crisis that Israel's religion underwent during the Babylonian exile and its aftermath, then (d) there certainly must be a mysticism generated from within Judaism. Moreover, this mysticism must have sustained not only marginal sects, but also the main religious leadership of the people. Furthermore, this Jewish mysticism must be found at a point in time not far from the period in which the reverberations of the aforementioned crises were absorbed. If these assumptions are not confirmed by historical research, it follows that the theory based on Scholem's basic intuition is incorrect.

Just as Scholem sought to discover the origins of mysticism in the earliest possible period, he also strove to follow the subsequent transformations of mysticism up to the latest possible period. He attempted to trace the thread of mysticism up to the threshold of modernity, and even beyond it, in such movements as Sabbatian-ism and its various transformations, Hassidism, and possibly even in the development of "utopian" messianism in Zionism.[33]

Scholem explicitly stated his belief that if the Jewish religion was to succeed in overcoming the crisis of modernity — which in his eyes was the most severe crisis ever encountered by Judaism — this would come about only through the renewal of a large mysti-cal movement. He knew how difficult and complicated such a feat would be, and he did not claim to know anything about the content and form of this mysticism. In his ironic way, he left the task of describing this mysticism to the prophets. He counted

---

33 Scholem dealt with this issue in his large book on Sabbatai Sevi, and also in a series of studies on Sabbatianism and Frankism. The question of the connection between Frankism and the *haskalah* is treated especially in the comprehensive study "The Career of a Frankist," in Hebrew, *Zion*, XXXV (1970).

himself among the company of professors who know nothing about the future.[34]

Nevertheless, Scholem's intense interest in the future is quite discernible in his work. With great suspense, Scholem pursues his search for the temporal boundaries of mysticism in Jewish history. This intensity seems to transform his scientific studies into a pulsating personal drama. This is the drama of the indefatigable explorer, the drama of the believer who seeks after a fascinating revelation in total confidence that the object of his quest truly exists.

In the process of his search, Scholem seems to be reenacting an experience resembling that of the mystic. But while the mystic strives to discover the secret of the deity, the scholar seeks to uncover the historical secret of mysticism, namely, the secret of its origin in the past and of its culmination in the days to come. Scholem worked extensively on the study of classical medieval *Kabbalah*. Still, his greatest energies were devoted to discovering the sources located on the borders of antiquity and modernity. These texts contained the enchanted secret of the beginning, the 'being' on the edge of 'nothingness,' and the enchanted secret of the future. A careful examination reveals that even in his research on medieval *Kabbalah*, Scholem first sought to uncover the secret origins of the *Zohar*, and later on, the secret of the origins of *Kabbalah*.[35] Similarly, in his research on the *Kabbalah* of Isaac Luria, he tries to unravel the secret origins of the Sabbatian movement, thereby uncovering the secret origins of the final stage beyond which lurks a future enveloped in total mystery. As a scholar Scholem may have remained within the "Professors'"

---

34 These doubts find expression in the essay "Reflections on the Possibility of Jewish Mysticism in Our Day." But Scholem also leaves room for the assumption that, beyond his doubts, lies a pulsating and firm belief that the source has not yet run dry. It is in this spirit that he ends the book *Major Trends*, as well as the later article "Reflections on Jewish Theology."

35 Scholem wrote a book entitled *The Origins of Kabbalah*, in Hebrew (Jerusalem and Tel-Aviv: Shocken, 1948). In the first chapter he asserts in a definitive manner, "The problem of the beginnings of the *Kabbalah* that was revealed in Jewish history at the start of the thirteenth century, is one of the most difficult problems of the history of Jewish religion, and certainly is one of its main problems" (p. 7).

limited range of operation, but the spiritual fervor poured into the concluding lines of his work *Major Trends in Jewish Mysticism* surely has a mystical foundation, if not a prophetic one.[36]

iv. Prophecy, Halakhah, and Philosophy

The assumption that mysticism is "the essence" of the Jewish religion also finds expression in Scholem's approach to religious manifestations that are not in themselves classified as mystical. Here it behooves us to consider three issues: first, Scholem's view of the religion unfolded in the biblical literature, and particularly his view of prophecy as religious experience; second, Scholem's concept of the religious content of a halakhic way of life; third, his view of philosophy in medieval times and the modern age.

With regard to the first of these three issues — and it must be admitted that this initially seems quite astonishing — we can say very little. Scholem did not devote a single study specifically to the development of Jewish religion in the biblical period, even though the application of his historical scheme demands such an investigation. What was the character of Jewish religion in its formative stage of "innocence"? Did it embody a myth, and if so, what was the content and character of this myth? What distinguishes the prophets' monotheism from polytheistic idolatry? What distinguishes between prophetic and priestly religion? When and how was the prophetic religion institutionalized? And finally, what is the relationship between the biblical religion and the earliest manifestations of Jewish mysticism?

It is astonishing that Scholem does not raise these questions. This is truly one of the major flaws in his philosophy of history. We will therefore return to this issue and deal with it extensively in the critical analysis that follows. At this juncture, however, all we can do is take note of several brief and incidental remarks which indicate that Scholem actually regards prophecy as the "innocent," primal, pre-institutional stage of the Jewish religion. Moreover, he

36 See *Major Trends*, pp. 349-50.

definitively states that prophecy does not fall within the category of mystical experience.[37] It further appears that in Scholem's scheme the Jewish religion that developed through a continuous and multi-faceted historical process up to the present day actually originated during the days of the second Temple. Only from that point does one find the rabbinic form of religion that can be called "Jewish religion." Does this mean that, in Scholem's view, biblical religion is actually detached from the historical progression of Judaism? If so, is Judaism's connection with Scripture nothing more than a myth? Scholem does not address these questions. The entire set of issues concerning the place of biblical religious experience within the history of the Jewish religion remains unclarified. The fact is that Scholem's historical research traces the origins of the Jewish religion only to the point from which one may begin to discuss Jewish mysticism, albeit on the basis of a few vague historical sources. Scholem's presupposition regarding the centrality of mysticism determined the parameters of his historical research.

We can speak more extensively on our second topic, Scholem's sense of the halakhic life's religious content, even though this issue also is not addressed in a systematic and comprehensive discussion. Scholem accepts the common assumption that *halakhah* is the institutional framework that preserved the unity of the Jewish religion and its continuity from the dawn of the second Temple period up to the present day. The fundamental belief in *"Torah from heaven"* is, in Scholem's opinion, the basis for the authentic continuity of the Jewish religion.[38] This belief is maintained in practice through a way of life that is governed by halakhic injunctions. Through the Sinaitic revelation, the *halakhah* derives authority that is renewed from one generation to the next.

---

37 These points are explicated particularly in the essay "Religious Authority and Mysticism" in *On the Kabbalah and Its Symbolism*, p. 9.
38 In several of his essays, Scholem repeatedly expresses this view in a definitive fashion. See especially "Reflections on the Possibility of Jewish Mysticism in Our Day" and "Reflections on Jewish Theology."

Scholem frequently stressed that the fundamental belief in "*Torah* from heaven" was central to Jewish mysticism as well. When he set out to address the question of whether a contemporary renewal of Jewish mysticism was possible, he asserted that the abundant doubts concerning this possibility derive from the fact that the fundamental belief in "*Torah* from heaven" has been undermined. In other words, the problem is that the source of *halakhah's* authority has been challenged. It is thus clear why Scholem included the affirmative attitude to halakhic obligation among the characteristics of Jewish mysticism even though, as we noted, he also saw fit to stress the antinomian tension embodied in mysticism, especially in its messianic utopianism.

The following matter requires careful consideration: despite the centrality of "*Torah* from heaven" in his conception of Judaism, Scholem seems to see the *halakhah* that bases itself on the myth of Sinaitic revelation as nothing other than an institutional framework. That is, Scholem sees *halakhah* merely in terms of an external framework, not a life-content that encompasses a religious experience with its own distinctive essence. There is only one short essay among the many long pieces written by Scholem in which he actually comes very close to recognizing the experiential content of the *halakhic* way of life, the essay "Three Types of Jewish Piety."[39] In this piece, Scholem sketches the portraits of "the rabbinic scholar" (*Talmid hakham*), "the just man" (*tzadik*) and "the pious man" (*Hassid*). This is perhaps the only essay in which Scholem does not rely upon a categorial scheme that includes mysticism as a central or necessary element. Nevertheless, it is astonishing that even in this essay, Scholem does not establish the simple fact that he is dealing with three models of halakhic piety. That is, he does not state that the *halakhah* represents both a framework and a content of direct and authentic religious experience.

Only the last of the three issues noted above is treated in a detailed and full-scale discussion. In this discussion, Scholem's

39 See *Explications and Implications*, pp. 541-9.

preference for mysticism is expressed in the most explicit fashion. Scholem found it necessary to deal with the subject of philosophy in the course of his intensive treatment of medieval mysticism. For medieval Jewish mysticism and medieval Jewish philosophy comprise twin religious movements that developed through a process of reciprocal influence and conflict. Scholem actually stressed the parallel influences of philosophy and mysticism on medieval religious creativity.[40]

Philosophy also attempted to cope reflexively with a deep religious crisis. This crisis was the result of the Jews' dispersion in a cultural-religious environment which undermined the validity of the *"Torah* of Israel." The feeling of *Hester Panim* (God's hiddenness) increased and ultimately damaged the intimate experiences of praying and studying *Torah*. Philosophy sought a solution to this problem through knowledge of systematic and comprehensive truth, for it was assumed that the determinism which manifests itself throughout the natural order is grounded in divine wisdom. Anyone who understands this determinism will accept reality as it is, as an expression of God's will or his governance. He will recognize that the achievement of divine presence consists only in comprehending the reality that is determined by God. Moreover, he will see that behavior governed by the laws of rationality constitutes the fulfillment of God's will and commandments. Retribution is immanent in good and bad deeds. This philosophical view thus seems to accept reality as it is given, while forsaking the basic myth of Jewish religion along with the hopes and expectations anchored in it.

The preceding analysis initially suggests that we are dealing with two parallel and opposing solutions. As noted above, however, there was actually a reciprocal influence between the two. Mysticism needs a comprehensive interpretation of reality; philos-

---

40 The contrast between the mystical approach and the philosophical approach in the middle ages is almost in the category of a methodological principle in Scholem's essays on central issues of Jewish thought. This kind of comparison is also found in the first lecture of *Major Trends*, and in all those essays devoted to the concept of redemption, as well as in the aforementioned essays dealing with the overall definition of mysticism.

ophy was the source available to the medieval kabbalists for this purpose. Mysticism does indeed strive to reach a hidden mythic stratum, but to reach this stratum, mysticism needs to use philosophy's conceptual scheme. With this scheme, it constructs a comprehensive interpretation of manifest reality. It is true that mysticism was more inclined toward the direction of Neoplatonic philosophy while the philosophers per se were inclined toward Aristotelianism, but in medieval times these two philosophical systems converged to a great extent, and various syntheses were created. In this way, a trace of mysticism managed to attach itself to philosophy, and more than a trace of philosophy filtered into mysticism. Several mystics even tried to offer a synthesis of mysticism and philosophy.

Scholem established all these facts in his scholarly studies, yet at the same time, he tended to emphasize the differences, rather than the parallels, between mysticism and philosophy. From Scholem's point of view, there was a decisive gap between (a) the authentic religious solution offered by mysticism, and (b) philosophy's artificial pseudo-solution which was essentially destined to fail. This distinction is merely derived from Scholem's a priori intuition concerning the nature of mysticism and the nature of philosophy as a phenomenon of spiritual life.

In Scholem's eyes mysticism is seen as religion in its process of regeneration, while philosophy is viewed, to begin with, as an outgrowth of a non-religious response to reality. For the philosopher believes that reality has no source beyond itself, and that the laws governing reality and lawfulness are necessary and immanent. Scholem in effect accepts the dichotomous choice between philosophy and religion as it is posed by R. Judah Halevi in the beginning of The Book of the *Kuzari*. On the one hand, there is the religious approach based on the believer's unmediated experience of divine presence. On the other hand, there is the rationalistic approach which does not recognize religious experience and therefore consists entirely in rational judgements pertaining to ordinary sensory experience.

42

As far as Scholem is concerned, the first approach is upheld by mysticism while the second is philosophical. The philosophical approach is defined by Scholem as non-religious from the very outset, even though philosophy can find a place for religion within the general scheme of things (usually, a place for religion will be found within the institutional realm of the state). It is therefore clear that philosophy cannot truly resolve the crisis of faith. At the very most, philosophy may suggest alternatives that resemble faith.

In Scholem's opinion, this dichotomy between philosophy and mysticism is apparent throughout all areas of religious activity. For example, if we consider the problem of the religious value of studying *Torah*, both mysticism and philosophy offer far-reaching methods of interpretation that carry the biblical texts beyond their plain meaning. The basis for these methods was found in the midrashic exegesis of the rabbinic sages. But the philosophers and mystics "opened up" the *midrash* in the most innovative and elaborate ways in order to find new, possibly even revolutionary truths which their forefathers had not fathomed. Of course there is a vast difference between the philosophical and mystical modes of interpretation. This difference finds expression both in vitality of content, and in the accuracy of the respective methods of interpretation. Mystical interpretation was symbolic, while philosophical interpretation was allegorical.[41]

Symbolic interpretation upholds the value of straightforward interpretation. Through the plain meaning of the text, symbolic interpretation seeks to uncover the hidden truth. The particular, literal form of the symbol is regarded as its necessary expression. No other expression could point to the hidden meaning. For this

---

41 The distinction between symbol and allegory is also a recurrent motif in Scholem's discussion of mysticism. This motif has the status of a methodological principle. The distinction is clearly tied in with a further distinction between (a) religiosity that is imbedded in myth, and (b) rationalistic religiosity which steers away from myth. Myth lives in symbols. Allegory is a tool for emptying the mythological content from ancient religious symbols. On this issue see especially *"Kabbalah* and Myth" in *On the Kabbalah and Its Symbolism.*

reason, there is a unique and absolute value to each letter, each word and each sentence in the sources.

By contrast, allegory treats words as exterior layers. These layers may have a certain independent value, but each of them is seen as an alterable symbol that can be replaced by a similar one. Indeed, the allegory is designed from the start to mask the writer's opinion and to point to it indirectly. The presupposition is that a more exact and adequate expression of the desired message exists, but for various reasons should not be used. Clearly, therefore, the philosophers who discover a web of Aristotelian or Platonic philosophical meditations in the writings of *Torah* and in the saying of the rabbinic sages are actually treating these texts and sayings as external veils. The knowledgeable few must lift and discard these veils in order to discover truth. There is neither a necessary linkage nor even a substantive connection between this truth and its expression in the sources.

We therefore find that the philosopher does not study *Torah*. He studies philosophy according to the philosophical route, while pretending to be studying *Torah*. This contrasts with the study of *Torah* through the symbolic route of mysticism. From the perspective of the believer-mystic, the newest and most courageous ideas truly erupt and emerge from the hidden depths of *Torah*. The mystic thus upholds the authority of prophetic revelation in total innocence and sincerity.

Scholem made similar observations concerning both the liturgy and the overall way of life defined by the injunctions of *Torah* or by the *halakhah*. Those who recite the standard prayers with the intention of the mystics treat every word and every sentence as a symbol containing hidden meanings. These meanings can be referred to only through the given words. When these words are pronounced with the proper intention, they elicit specific activities in the higher and lower spheres. The same applies to fulfillment of the *Torah*'s injunctions. In order for the fulfillment of an ordinance to serve its function in the higher spheres, it is necessary to pay attention to the precise details of each ordinance and to obey the commandments with the proper intention. Consequently, the mystic preserves the halakhic medium with great care, and infuses it with a new and vital content. The same cannot be said of the philosopher, as portrayed by Scholem. As far as the philosophers are concerned, prayers and ritualistic ordinances are merely external, pedagogical devices designed to equip the believer to fulfill the true objective, rational examination leading to knowledge of eternal truth. There is no essential connection between this objective and the prayers or the practical ordinances. We thus find that, for the ideal philosopher, prayers and ordinances are superfluous devices. If he makes use of them, it is only for political-pedagogical reasons. So once again, philosophy offers an illusory substitute for the religious way of life.

Scholem thus tilted the scales in favor of mysticism and against philosophy. This maneuver directly affected his attitude to Judaic thought and scholarship in the modern era. In effect, he dismissed *Wissenschaft des Judentums* of the nineteenth century and all of modern Jewish theology for the same reasons which led him to deny the religious authenticity of Maimonides' work. In Scholem's view, all of these works exhibited a rationalistic tendency which, of course, rejects mysticism.[42] As far as Scholem is concerned, rationalism and the denial of mysticism actually represent inauthentic religion. As a matter of course, this type of religion leads Judaism so far astray it threatens to end the continuous existence of a distinctive Judaism.

It will be necessary to examine these views in greater detail in the critical discussion which follows. Before turning to this discussion, however, it behooves us to offer a brief summary of Scholem's theory as a whole. According to Scholem the history of the Jewish religion actually dates from the start of the second Temple period. He employs a historical scheme based on the definition of mysticism as a particular stage in the development of

---

42 See the well known and highly influential essay "Reflections on *Wissenschaft des Judentums*" in *Explications and Implications*, pp. 385-403. These views are mentioned incidentally in several other articles.

each religion. According to this scheme, prophetic religion is seen as a stage of pre-mystical innocence. If we follow Scholem's ideas to their logical conclusions, it turns out that there is no real continuity between the innocent, prophetic stage and the halakhic-rabbinic religion. The halakhic-rabbinic religion, which is internally imbued with mystical movements, reached its present incarnation by way of many transformations.

In any case, we can state the following with certainty: the Jewish religion that Scholem examines is primarily rabbinic Judaism, the product of the scribes (*Soferim*), the palestinian sages of the Mishnaic period (*Tannaim*), and their successors within the traditions and literature of Oral *Torah*. This Jewish, traditional-rabbinic religion originates as such during the dawn of the Second Temple period. Although Scholem does not say so explicitly, his writings imply the following: when the first rabbinic sages appealed to Scripture, they were appealing to an earlier stage located beyond the range of their own rabbinic Judaism. Scholem further suggests that the emergence of Jewish mysticism was already inherent in the original stance of the founders of rabbinic Judaism.

Scholem believes that Jewish mysticism derives from an internal, independent source. Although he recognizes that Jewish mysticism absorbed many external influences, Scholem is inclined to assume that during the span of time between the third and first centuries B.C.E., a mystical movement arose within Judaism. This movement was not merely a marginal sect. Rather, it developed within the very heart of institutional rabbinic (halakhic) Judaism. It expresses the religious experience of figures who played a central role in the formation of the halakhic tradition. One therefore cannot comprehend their activities — even in the manifest realms of *halakhah* and *aggadah* — except in connection with the latent realms of their worldview and experience. From this period onward, the development of the Jewish religion must be observed as a movement on two parallel and contiguous tracks: manifest *Torah* and latent *Torah*.

46

In any case, mystical movements are certainly active throughout Judaism's progression, although we cannot always gain a complete and clear perception of these movements. These movements are dynamic. They undergo transformations, and from time to time, one discerns a new beginning. One such nascence involves the *Kabbalah* originating in Southern France and Spain at the end of the twelfth and the beginning of the thirteenth centuries. Another example of a new beginning is Lurianic *Kabbalah* of the sixteenth century. It may also be correct to regard Hassidim as such an original movement. In any case, it is clear that mysticism is essentially a daring, revolutionary, regenerating movement, because it reaches out toward the primordial experience of presence before the divinity. For this reason, mysticism has many faces and a multitude of incarnations. Nevertheless, mysticism preserves a traditional thread of continuity with the internal core of the Jewish religion's institutional framework, namely the halakhic framework that is based on the fundamental belief in *"Torah* from heaven."

One may thus say that, according to Scholem, mysticism as defined above is the source of the Jewish religion's vitality. This is, first and foremost, because mysticism embodies the creative-religious motivation of the great leaders and shapers of the Jewish tradition in its manifest realm. But Scholem maintains no less emphatically that mysticism, despite its esoteric nature, should be seen as the source that enriches popular religion. Although this process may not be apparent in the ancient periods, it is clear that in the aftermath of the Spanish expulsion, the *Kabbalah* spread to a wide range of Jewish circles. Moreover, after the creation of Lurianic *Kabbalah* in the sixteenth century, mysticism became so widespread that it actually became the mass religion of the Jews. This provided the background for the daring Sabbatian movement and also for Hassidism.

Scholem bitterly rejected the efforts of Jewish theologians and modern scholars who suggested dogmatic definitions of Judaism.[43] As a matter of principle, he insisted that Judaism is a wide and open spectrum spanning the creations of the Jewish people. As such, Judaism includes many different spiritual movements. Sometimes, the ideas of one movement contradict those of another. However, together with this assertion, or perhaps in spite of it, one finds in Scholem's essays several assumptions that demarcate the historical Jewish religion and unify it through several basic distinctive characteristics.[44]

Externally, Judaism is delimited by the boundaries of institutional *halakhah*, which is based on the fundamental belief in the tenet of "*Torah* from Heaven." Internally, Judaism is an inventive mystical experience that is well-anchored in a tradition and faithful to the authority of a tradition that, in turn, is anchored in revelation. To be sure, Scholem does not deny that non-mystical currents are part of the multi-faceted unity of Judaism. Nevertheless, the fact is that he had a negative attitude to non-mystical trends. This applies both to strictly institutional-halakhic currents as well as to philosophical ones. Scholem dismissed them as essentially inauthentic.

By contrast, he saw the antinomian phenomena of Jewish mysticism as an authentic dialetical expression of the messianic-utopian and spontaneous-experiential dimensions of Jewish mysticism. Under this rubric, he also included the destructive antinomian outburst of Sabbatianism and its Frankist incarnation. The religious anarchism of these movements illustrates the crisis of the encounter with modernity. The signs of crisis emerge precisely from within the mythic depths that comprise religion's source of vitality. In Sabbatianism and its transformations, the ruins of an

---

43 As a rule, Scholem mentions these points in the context of arguments against the modern definitions of Judaism. See for example the essay "Reflections on *Wissenschaft des Judentums*."

44 Scholem's most extensive attempt to define the permanent and unifying characteristics of Judaism appears in his comprehensive essay "Reflections of Jewish Theology."

infrastructure were revealed. An authentic solution can be generated only from this infrastructure.

For this reason, Scholem endeavored to uncover the hidden transformations of Sabbatianism, not only among those who remained faithful to Sabbatianism, but also in those movements that coped with the crisis in a positive fashion, i.e., Hassidism and the *Haskalah*. This led him to his major conclusion regarding contemporary religious Jewish thought: one must not place one's faith in efforts to remodel the Jewish religion solely upon its halakhic or dogmatic institutions. Mysticism alone can generate a solution that is at once both truly new and also an authentic continuation of the tradition. At the same time, however, Scholem concedes that the problem of renewing mysticism in our times raises doubts upon doubts. Even so, for those in search of paths for contemporary Judaism, Scholem offers only one bit of advice: engage in an empathetic study of Jewish mysticism throughout the generations, and look forward with hope.

Although these views contain many unclear and equivocal points, they are stated in sharp language and with authoritative force. There is no doubt that they exerted an influence on the programmatic views of contemporary Jewish scholarship and religious thought.[45] Consequently, this outlook must be subjected to a thorough critical examination.

---

45 See, for example, Joseph Dan, "Mysticism in Jewish History, Religion and Literature" in *Studies in Jewish Mysticism* (n.p.: AJS, 1938).

PART 2.
CRITICAL DISCUSSION

CHAPTER 2

THE DEFINITION OF MYSTICISM:

PRESUPPOSITIONS OF SCHOLEM'S DEFINITION

A thorough critical discussion of Scholem's views must focus initially on the presuppositions behind his definition of mysticism. Is mysticism truly a necessary stage in the development of each religion? Is mysticism indeed a necessary stage within the Jewish religion, or at least within the major current that distinguished Judaism from the other religions in its environment, from the period of the prophets up to the present? Our answers to these questions tend to differ from those of Scholem. But clearly, in order to substantiate our position, we must first assess Scholem's definition of mysticism, and the historical scheme it implies.

The definition proposed by Scholem is based on the comparative research of mystical phenomena in various religions. His definition includes two elements accepted by most scholars of mysticism: (a) mysticism is a late development in the history of a religion. Mysticism is reflexive. It stands in a dialectical tension with the institutional-normative religion within which it develops. (b) the phenomenon of mysticism should not be isolated from the other characteristics of the religion that serves as its matrix. One should not speak of a single "pure mysticism" that can be "refined" from the "crude elements" of various religions. There are diverse types of mysticism. These are distinguished from one another by the very same elements that differentiate the religions which constitute the matrices of the various mysticisms.

However, Scholem further claims that one cannot propose a single definition for the phenomenon called "mysticism" in the various religions -and in this regard, he opposes the opinion prevailing among most scholars of mysticism. To Scholem, each mysticism, by definition, has distinctive characteristics. Therefore, the only common element shared by all phenomena called "mysticism" is their specific place within the tripartite scheme of the development of religions. Mysticism is the reflexive stage that expresses the believers' longing to return to the stratum of mythic innocence after a religion has undergone the process of institutionalization and its inherent crises.

Scholem's radical argument does not withstand critical evaluation. Indeed, his assertion flies in the face of other descriptions of mysticism in Scholem's own essays. Scholem ends up presupposing that mysticism can be characterized by a particular set of features which together comprise a crystalized and definitive spiritual disposition.

Among these definitive dispositional characteristics are the following:

1. At the foundation of any mystical religion lies an awareness of a necessary contradiction deriving from the nature of the universe, and of corporeal man. The contradiction is between (a) the mode and content of man's ordinary experience through sensory impressions and cognitive judgements, and (b) the mode and content of man's experience in the realm that includes a supernatural, divine presence.

2. All mystical religion rests on the basic assumption that one needs to overcome the limitations of physical perception in order to cope with the crisis stemming from the natural status and condition of man. One must transcend the contours of the portrait of the cosmos as perceived by the senses. One must reach another realm of reality. This is a higher and more internal realm which cannot be perceived either by the senses or by a mind that functions on the basis of sensory impressions.

3. Any mystical religion is founded upon the assumption that the beliefs and dictates of religion relate to two realms of human reality, a manifest external-earthly realm, and a latent internal-spiritual realm. Furthermore, there is a tension between these two realms. They conceal or even contradict one another. Consequently, mystical knowledge and experience is the exclusive province of a select few. Only through these extraordinary

individuals can the influence of mystical experience trickle down to ordinary persons.

4. All mystical religions rest on the basic need to develop a special technique in order to overcome the bifurcation between the terrestrial and the extra-terrestrial. This technique, a meditational prayer or another ritualistic medium, is based on a highly detailed, esoteric knowledge of the hidden connection between the terrestrial and extra-terrestrial realms.[46]

The presence of these general characteristics in mysticism does not challenge the correct assertion that there is no "pure" universal mysticism. Each mysticism depicts, in its own way, the various realms of reality as well as the laws which govern these realms, the connections between them, and so forth. Each mysticism has its own means of migrating from one realm to another. Likewise, each mysticism has its own mode of perceiving the mystical experience that constitutes its *telos*. To be sure, these differences derive from the specific content and the distinctive history of the particular religion within which each mysticism developed. But for our purposes, it is important to scrutinize the characteristics of mystical phenomena as such. This examination produces the following qualification: not every reflexive response to the crisis of innocent religion necessarily belongs within the category of mysticism.

There may be forms of reflexive response that do not generate the aforementioned dichotomy between earthly and spiritual reality. There may be responses that do not require one to overcome the limitations of corporeal existence and to transcend the portrait of the universe perceived through man's ordinary sensations and cognitive judgements. Some responses may not generate a ritualistic technique designed to blaze a pathway from the inferior realm of reality to the supreme one.

There may be forms of response which direct man toward a deeper understanding of our world and of his connection with the God of our universe without removing him from the universe and

46 See the aforementioned essays dealing with Scholem's definition of mysticism (cf. footnote no. 1).

its lawfulness through ecstasy or meditation. And if there are such responses, it may be that already, at the stage of innocent religion, one can distinguish between those religions in which the mystical response is essentially inherent and those in which it is not. In other words, it is not sufficient to distinguish between different forms of mysticism on the basis of the link between each mysticism and the religious matrix within which it is generated. We also need to distinguish between religions in which mysticism inheres, and those in which the development of mysticism is entirely foreign to their nature.

Indeed, we wish to argue, and to demonstrate in the subsequent discussion, that in the Jewish religion, which underwent monumental crises during its long history, there have been many non-mystical responses to crisis. Moreover, the non-mystical response is actually the most common and prevailing reaction. Under no circumstances is it correct to characterize the non-mystical response merely as "institutional" and ossified. On the contrary, the non-mystical response is vital and regenerating. So far as this is true, one may assume that the non-mystical response is somehow embedded in a feature that has distinguished the Jewish religion from its point of inception.

In short, then, mysticism itself actually appeared as a marginal phenomenon in Jewish history. At the dawn of the modern era, this phenomenon did indeed become widespread. But one may not portray mysticism as a manifestation deriving necessarily from the distinctive essence of the Jewish religion, nor may one portray mysticism as the source from which the Jewish religion renews itself from one generation to the next.

CHAPTER 3

MYSTICISM IN ANCIENT JUDAISM

i. Jewish Gnosis and Non-Mystical Religion

The preceding discussion indicates the need for a more detailed study. We must explore several issues that Scholem failed to address with the thoroughness required by the basic historical-philosophical generalization that he posits in his own scholarly studies. As we recall, Scholem sought to prove that a mystical movement already existed in Judaism at the dawn of the Tannaite era. He further claimed that within the ranks of this mystical movement, one may identify some of the seminal figures who created and modeled "Pharisaic," or Rabbinic Judaism. More-over, Scholem wished to prove that this mystical movement, which is referred to in the scientific jargon as "Jewish Gnosis," is not (as many scholars believe) the product of external influence. Rather, this movement was generated by an internal development within the Jewish religion.

Some of Scholem's most prominent students go so far as to speak of a direct continuity between "Jewish Gnosis" and certain chapters of the biblical literature.[47] These scholars locate the origins of Jewish mysticism in the biblical period. Their opinion seems to be the guiding trend of current research on Jewish mysticism during the period of the second Temple. Previous generations of scholars tended to assume that "Jewish Gnosis" is a product of external, pagan influences. But today, most scholars agree that there is no evidence of external influence. The development of "Jewish Gnosis" from an independent Jewish source thus seems more likely.

In response to the prevalent viewpoint, we must first point out that the scholarly status of research in this field is far from clear. No scholar has yet succeeded in providing a documented and compelling description of the development of "Jewish Gnosis"

47 See Ithamar Gruenwald, *Apocalyptic and Merkavah Mysticism* (Leiden: Kln, 1980).

within the context of the fundamental problems of the Israelite people and religion during the early second Temple period. This failure should come as no surprise. The documentary evidence is scarce and the relevant sources are fragmented and unintelligible. Although the condition of the historical evidence has been improved somewhat lately, we still remain mostly in the dark.

Any assumptions concerning the origins of "Jewish Gnosis," and especially assumptions concerning the internal and external factors stimulating its development, are still in the category of hypotheses. They will remain hypothetical conjectures in the future as well. Such hypotheses are profoundly influenced by the typo-logical-philosophical theories prevailing among scholars. In any case, it seems that the issue of typology remains primary and most significant. Let us assume that the currently prevalent hypothesis is correct. That is, let us assume that "Jewish Gnosis" developed independently in Jewish circles during the early part of the second Temple period. Let us further postulate that this circle of believers derived its major motifs from biblical literature. We may even grant that the biblical corpus already contained many distinct mystical motifs. (The present author believes that there are in fact such motifs in the biblical text, and although marginal, they were necessary footholds for the development of a mysticism entrenched in the Jewish tradition.)

But even if we accept all of the above assumptions, have we thereby understood the cultural-historical motivation underlying the development of "Jewish Gnosis"? Have we excluded the possibility that the challenge of polytheistic religions was a deter-minative influence upon an internal development of the Jewish religion? Is there any basis for denying the existence of external polytheistic influences within the biblical corpus itself? Should we not regard these influences as the source of mystical motifs that constantly resurface in Jewish trends of the second Temple period?

The fundamental question may be stated as follows: within the spectrum of diverse and opposing religious trends found in Juda-ism of the biblical and second Temple periods, what constitutes the core that distinguishes toraitic-prophetic monotheism? Furthermore, what renders toraitic-prophetic monotheism a conscious adversary of polytheistic religions and their rituals and even of those polytheistic tendencies that the Israelite prophets found within their own culture? How does mysticism relate to this core of Jewish monotheism? How did this monotheism develop? How did it draw upon the biblical sources? How exactly did it develop in relation to internal and external religious trends, both mystical and non-mystical, since the early days of the second Temple?

To deal with this issue adequately, it is thus necessary to explore the scholarly research on the Israelite religion during the biblical era. Specifically, one must examine research dealing with the characteristics that distinguish prophetic belief from polytheistic religions. In particular, one must examine the role and nature of myth in prophetic belief. Are we dealing here simply with a stage of "innocent religion"? Does the effort to cope with the crisis of innocent religion specifically require the development of mysticism?

A second issue to be examined in detail is the relation between religious, mystical works created from the Second Temple period onward and non-mystical, manifestly religious works created by those numerous sages whose universe contains no traces of mysticism at all. (After considering Scholem's views, we ought to stress that the number of these sages — among whom one can identify figures of central importance — is far from negligible.) Further participants in the process of non-mystical religious creation are those sages who were indeed mystics, but whose mystical experience did not find expression in the realm of their manifest creations. (To this category belong most of the sages who had personal leanings toward mysticism.) To begin with, we must ask ourselves, what is the nature of this non-mystical religious creation? In what tradition is it anchored? Does it really depend on mysticism as its latent dimension? Or does this type of creation stand independently, and does it have a certain completeness in its own right? If so, are we truly dealing merely with an "institutional" religion, or does this religion of *Torah* and divine injunctions possess a rich, thriving and regenerating content of experience and belief. Is it perhaps in this religion, rather than in mysticism, that one finds the authentic continuation of the element that has distinguished the Jewish religion since its original biblical manifestation?

A final problem needing clarification is the intense, inner tension which accompanies mystical movements when they appear in Judaism. This tension is linked to a strong awareness of the danger that mysticism poses for believers who become involved in it and for the overall religious faith of those who do not belong to the inner circle entrusted with secret doctrines. Scholem claims that this tension characterizes the relation between mysticism and any institutional religion within which it develops. For this reason, says Scholem, mysticism is generally esoteric. By its very nature, mysticism is a "secret" doctrine which is to be revealed only to worthy persons.

At this point, it is worth recalling the methodological principle of Scholem himself. He states that one should examine each phenomenon of mysticism in its own right, while seeking its affinity with the institutional religion within which it developed. Does this principle not apply to assessments of the essential relation between institutionalized religion and the secret doctrines of mysticism? Does one find in every religion a tension of the same character and intensity? Does one find in all religions the same degree of personal and public danger? Did mysticism end up producing the same destructive results in all religions?

In a word, should we not posit a distinction between (a) religions in which mysticism functions as an integral part of the religion's structure and content (despite, or even by virtue of the tension inherent in the function of mysticism), and (b) religions for which the supplement of mysticism constitutes an essentially alien element. As for the latter, may one say that even if mysticism satisfies a deep need of a certain class of believers, it does not function as an integral part of the religion's structure and content, but rather as an element that supplements or transcends them?

Thus, is there not a danger that, under certain circumstances, mysticism will act against, and threaten to destroy, the structure and content of these religions?

ii. The Distinctive Character of Biblical Religion

As mentioned above, the question of the character of the Israelite religion during the biblical period and its place in the development of the Jewish religion remains unclarified throughout the works of Scholem In general terms, we deduced from his writings that he does not detect mysticism within the prophetic teaching, and that he includes expressions of the biblical worldview and way of life within the stage of innocent religion. On second thought, perhaps it is not surprising that these points were not stated by Scholem in a clear and crystalized fashion. Scholem surely was aware of the elaborate scholarly research indicating that, already during the biblical era, there were various trends and developments, as well as major conflicts, within the Israelite religion. Can one seriously argue that the Israelite religion did not undergo processes of institutionalization long before the Babylonian exile and the return to Zion? Can one seriously argue that the Jewish religion did not already confront major crises of faith which required a reflexive approach during the height of the Second Temple period? And, if the development of mysticism is indeed necessary in such situations, should we not expect to find mystical thought within the very core of the biblical literature itself?

It is thus possible that Scholem refrained from writing in an orderly and crystalized fashion about the Israelite religion during the biblical period because he recognized the major difficulties inherent in this issue. It may be that Scholem preferred to leave this issue to those who specialize in biblical research, so he himself might concentrate on the scholarly gulf within which he wished to confine himself. But there may be another reason that led Scholem to refrain from clarifying this issue even on the level of a historical-philosophical discussion. Perhaps it was the fact that such a discussion would have placed Scholem in a face-to-face confrontation with the works of Jewish philosophers and theologians of the nineteenth and twentieth centuries, and would have forced him to abandon his sweeping rejection, and to enter a substantive, detailed theological and historical-philosophical debate. For, as far as its literary moorings are concerned, modern Jewish thought is based primarily on Scripture, on a phenomenology of religious faith in the biblical period, and especially a phenomenology of the prophetic teaching. This is perhaps the most serious and important substantive scholarly contribution of modern Jewish religious thought.[48] Thus, if Scholem had addressed this issue, he also would have had to stringently test his main intuition, that which led him to his elaborate re search on Jewish mysticism in the first place. For his intuition would have been confronted on one flank by the scientific research of biblical literature, and on the other flank by contemporary Jewish thought. It is therefore possible that he did not desire such a confrontation while he was caught up in the full momentum of his research.

But whatever may be the reasons for Scholem's choice to avoid this set of issues, it is clear that those who follow in his wake must examine the validity of his historical-philosophical presupposition. This requires us to cross the boundaries Scholem set up for himself, and to rely upon a phenomenological examination of Israelite religion's content during the biblical period.

From our present deliberation's perspective, we can point to two schools that cut across the various groups of scholars studying the phenomenology of Israelite religion during the biblical period.

The first school portrays the appearance of Israelite religion, along with the distinctive characteristics that set it apart from the polytheistic religions of Eastern Asia, as an original revolution

48 The appeal to Scripture as a primary source for the development of Jewish theology can already be discerned in the work of Moses Mendelsohn. This is also a salient feature that runs through the thought of all the theologians belonging to the reform trend, people such as Formschecther, Samuel Hirsch, Geiger, Phillipson and Kohler. This line of thought was also preserved in the theology generated within the reformist trend of the twentieth century. Thus, the works of Hermann Cohen, Franz Rosenzweig and Martin Buber rely particularly upon Scripture.

against polytheistic religion. Such a revolution may have occurred against the backdrop of a spiritual crisis that took place within one of the polytheistic religions and led to the creation of a new religion.[49] According to this school of thought, Israelite religion is to be categorized as a nascent religion. But this new beginning also grew out of a context of previous development and a background of crisis. Consequently, this religion is far from the innocence that may be attributed to the very ancient religions.

The second school of thought depicts the Israelite-biblical religion as an original phenomenon that shares no substantive link with the earlier polytheistic religions.[50] In other words, according to this school, polytheism provides neither a backdrop nor a point of origin for the development of Israelite religion. Rather, this religion should be seen as the flash of an initial insight which was isolated from its cultural environment and which developed from within its distinctive conceptual and emotional milieu. Only after it had been crystalized did it face the crucial confrontation with polytheistic religions. This second viewpoint does indeed enable us to describe a stage of religious innocence in Israelite religion. It is interesting, however, that even according to this school of thought, the development beyond the stage of religious innocence does not lead in the direction of mysticism. Proponents of this view regard the initial insight expressed in biblical religion as alien to mysticism. In its very essence, biblical religion turns away from the direction of mysticism. This implies, therefore, that the difference between the Israelite religion and the neighboring polytheistic religions is already discernible at the stage of religious innocence. This distinction determines different courses of development. While the polytheistic religions may be essentially oriented in the direction of mysticism, Israelite religion is essentially oriented in a

49 Within the realm of the Jewish-philosophical interpretation of Scripture, this approach is represented by Hermann Cohen, Franz Rosenzweig and Martin Buber. This approach is based upon a view accepted by most biblical scholars.

50 The most salient and consistent proponent of this approach is Yehezkel Kaufmann. See his summary of his own viewpoint under the heading "The Religion of Israel" in the Biblical Encyclopedia (Hebrew).

different direction, one which is distinct from mysticism and alien to it.

It thus transpires that as far as their approach to mysticism is concerned, the two schools of thought stand in parallel agreement. Israelite religion is unique, because it bears witness to the revelation of a single God who is not one of the forces of nature, but rather a supernatural personality ruling the forces of nature. Since this solitary God is not one of the forces of nature, he is not influenced by those natural impulses which affect the polytheistic deities. One must not appeal to this God through temptation or magical invocation. This God manifests a moral concern for man and the world. He demands from man loyalty and devotion. These are expressed by man's obedience to his commandments. The fulfillment of man's needs is therefore contingent upon loyalty and obedience to God.

Against this background, the experience of presence before God takes on a character entirely different from polytheistic epiphany. The presence of God can indeed be felt within the creature who obeys him. But God himself is not seen, and his essence is not known by man. Only the word of God is heard by man. Only God's will, or his commandments, are revealed to man. When man becomes conscious of God's commands, and subsequently obeys them, he feels the presence of God as a sensation of love reciprocated through love. Obviously, certain events in nature and history (including both those interpreted as reward and grace and those interpreted as punishment) provide more tangible evidence of this divine presence. But it must be emphasized that, to begin with, we are speaking of presence before an entity standing beyond human vision and comprehension. At the same time, however, we are dealing with a network of relations actualized within the realm of the human being's natural and historical reality. God relates to this reality as creator, leader, legislator, executor of retribution, and redeemer. Man thus experiences the presence of his hidden God throughout the full range of his manifest world. This dialectic of the hidden within the manifest and the manifest within the hidden characterizes the religion of the prophets from the moment it first appears.[51]

Such religious intuitions contain at their very base a reflexive aspect. They require a particular kind of conscious relation to unmediated experience in the given world. It is written in Psalm 19, "The heavens declare the glory of god, and the firmament recites his handiwork." Ostensibly, this is a simple and direct expression of enthusiasm regarding the majesty of the cosmos. Actually, it is an enthusiastic reflection on the glory hidden in the revealed world and the elements expressed through it. The manifest heavens attest to the glory of the hidden God whose benevolent will constitutes the sole reason for the regeneration of the universe. This is a reflexive experience. But we are not dealing here with a philosophical reflection, nor with a mystical one. For the thought and feeling do not burst forth beyond the natural-terrestrial sphere of man. Rather the thought and feeling here expressed depict the metaphysical dimension as God's willful-moral relation to man's ordinary existence in the world.

If, over the course of its history, each religion suffers a crisis with regard to the experience of unmediated presence before God, then from the very outset, this crisis is embedded in Israelite religion as it is depicted above. For, from the beginning Israelite religion recognizes the possibility that God's appeal to man and man's appeal to God will go unanswered and will not result in proximity. The meeting of God and man is not a necessary fact. Neither is it a necessary result of certain rituals. Since the relation is intentional and ethical, it is presupposed that God or man may refuse to heed the call of the other, and they may conceal their faces from one another.

This affects Scripture's definition of faith's parameters. The Bible's concern is to establish trust on the basis of moral certainty, without depending on any external assurances. In a relationship

---

51 This is based upon the view of the scholars mentioned above. A clear and exhaustive statement of this position appears in Julius Guttmann's *History of Jewish Philosophy*, in Hebrew (Jerusalem: Bialik, 1911), in the chapter on the main ideas of biblical religion. See page 11ff.

based on this type of faith, the believer is certain that, when necessary, God will stand by the man who fulfills divine injunctions. But this certainty is coupled with an acceptance of the possibility that the believer who is sure of his own righteousness will not be redeemed. In this case, the believer will have to decipher and make sense of his situation.

Does this type of religious outlook have a stage of primal innocence? The answer to this question is not as simple as the preceding analysis would suggest. From scholarly research regarding the religion of the prophets and the history of post-biblical Israelite religion, we learn that the institutions of Israelite religion underwent far-reaching changes as a result of major crises.

There are noticeable differences between the experience of divine presence as described by the early prophets and the very same experience as described by the later prophets. And there is certainly a difference between the experience of divine presence attained by the prophets and that attained by the sages during the period of the second Temple. The sages' religious consciousness distinguishes clearly between times when God's visage is revealed *(gilui panim)* and times when it is concealed *(kisui panim)*. There are times when Israel's people and its leaders live with the feeling that God resides among them, and guides them through the winding path of historical trials and tribulations. Whenever the word of God is needed, it is heard from the mouths of prophets. At these times, the sacrifices and prayers are accepted graciously and elicit a positive response. But there are times when the word of God is not heard, when the sacrifices and prayers do not elicit a response.

This belief is surely the product of something inherent in the nature of the Israelite people's historical experience. And indeed, one can find in Israelite annals a basis for the construction of a historical scheme that distinguishes between (a) the state of religious innocence and (b) situations of crisis that call for an ever-deepening reflexive response. Furthermore, one must not rule out the possibility that the crisis will be responded to by mysticism.

The fact is that in several instances, there was indeed a response through mysticism to the crisis of faith. It may even be that the experiences of several prophets fall in this category. Perhaps their visions could therefore serve as "natural" objects for later mystical interpretations.[52] Nevertheless, our preceding analysis clearly suggests the following conclusion: the turn toward mysticism cannot be seen as inherent in the nature of the prophetic religion; mysticism is not the essential self-expression of this religion, nor can it be depicted as a necessary response to religious crisis.

Indeed, the contrary may be the case. Even in the stage of religious innocence, there is a reflexive element in the Israelite religion which is not mystical. Moreover, even at this early stage, Israelite religion manifests an awareness that God may conceal his visage. Perhaps this implies that atonement is the appropriate response to a crisis induced by the concealment of God's visage. Atonement, in the sense taught by the prophets, means to purify one's heart and to mend one's ways. One must experience remorse for one's sins, renounce them, and perform deeds that find favor in God's eyes. It goes without saying that through these actions, the original innocence is also shattered. The path of atonement requires an ever-deepening reflexive effort on man's part. This effort is directed toward an understanding of one's self and one's motives, as well as of God's injunctions and of the manner of observing them. It is also directed toward comprehending the ways and ends of God's governance.

Mature religious thought is no longer satisfied with the simple answers of innocent religion. The heart of man is deep and circuitous; the routes of history are complex. The more these complexities are discovered, the more it becomes clear that the fulfillment of divine dictates is a matter requiring an even greater

52 *Maaseh Merkavah* is the secret contained in those chapters in Ezekiel and Isaiah which describe the appearance of God on his throne or chariot. These descriptions are on the border of epiphany. The issue of whether they constitute actual epiphanies remains complex and controversial. But in any case, they provide a foothold for mystical visions that fall within the category of epiphany. For this reason, the *Merkavah* depictions are central to the various currents of mysticism in Judaism.

measure of spiritual, intentional and conceptual effort. This kind of deep, reflexive religious thought can already be found in the various layers of biblical writings, not to mention in the thought of Jewish sages in late antiquity and the middle ages.[53] But this reflexive deepening of thought does not necessarily entail either penetration into a higher realm of reality or an apocalyptic conception of history. In situations of extreme suffering, religious persons may be tempted to turn toward mysticism. But mysticism is not the only solution. Furthermore, mysticism does not constitute a solution that flows from the fundamental tenets of prophetic religion. Indeed, the contrary is the case. Mysticism turns out to be an aberration. Moreover, mysticism inherently contains the danger of producing a spiritual crisis more severe than the crisis which initially posed the challenge that generated its development.

---

53 The contrast between the earlier and later prophetic books, as well as the contrast between the prophetic books and the books of Writings *(Ketuvim)*, especially the Book of Job, reveals how far biblical religious thought stands from naivete with respect to God's leadership and providence over human beings. This issue is a source of constant deliberation. However, this struggle does not lead necessarily to mystical solutions.

CHAPTER 4

THE HISTORICAL MYTH OF THE JEWISH RELIGION

i. Myth and De-mythologization

The preceding analysis suggests the following: if mysticism is to be portrayed as a solution called for by the substantial essence of a primal religious experience, then one must stipulate that this is not a "rule" applying to all religions. Rather, we are dealing with a "rule" that applies only to a particular type of religion. It applies only to religions that have an original and primal myth which already embodies a total picture of the universe. This total picture must include divine forces or gods as part of the complete universe, although they may be ranked in a hierarchy.

These kinds of religions directly express the human wish to decode the universe's secret. The myth deciphers the essence of the cosmos, its components, and the necessary and causal relations which govern the universe and determine its properties. This effort is designed to give man maximal control over the forces upon which his fate is predicated. Man is thereby able to direct the procedures of nature in a way that benefits the fulfillment of his yearnings.

These religions are essentially oriented toward epiphany. By epiphany, we mean an experience through which the gods reveal their nature or substantial essence to human beings. The myth of these religions in its earliest and most naive formulations already expresses the epiphany of the gods. In some instances, nature is portrayed as a manifestation of the essence of gods. In other instances, we find depictions of gods whose distinct nature stands above the sphere of ordinary natural forces. But in either case, the myth conveys the message of a knowledge that enables man to manipulate the gods to his own benefit through deeds which either fulfill their needs or constrain their natural inclinations.

Obviously, a breakdown in the ritualistic "efficiency" of this type of religion will naturally awaken a reflexive effort to discover

69

the cause of failure. The effort will seek a deeper understanding of the "nature" of the gods and their mode of action in terrestrial reality. If something essential has eluded man, and its lack predicates failure, the believers must penetrate the nature of the gods, the world, and man who mediates between these two. This indeed generates the mystical response delineated in Scholem's definition. So at the moment of crisis, mysticism presents itself as an option for the type of polytheistic religion described above. This point is verified by plain historical facts. It was the polytheistic religions that served as fertile ground for mysticism's development. In Judaism, by contrast, mysticism was for the most part imported. The label on this "import" was altered in order to render it acceptable for public use.[54]

Another independent set of issues is raised by the following questions. First, did Israelite religion possess a myth from the time of its inception? If so, was this myth capable of constituting a foothold for mystical religious influences? Among the scholars of biblical theology also, these questions The discussion of this issue has recently been summarized by Benjamin Oppenheimer in his article "Biblical Theology and Monotheistic Myth," Immanuel, No. 14 (1982), pp. 7-26. remain the focus of sustained controversy.[55]

54 As noted above, we must leave the question of the origins of "Jewish Gnosis" in the category of issues requiring further examination. Those mystical movements whose origins have been clarified and which have been deciphered through historical research, have all turned out to be products of external influence, whether it is the mystical neo-platonic influence of Plotinus, or an Islamic Sufi influence, or the influence of mystical movements in the Christian world. It is true that the Kabbalists imagined that they possessed a tradition or a direct revelation from above. It is also true that the external influences underwent a process of reshaping and adaptation to the Jewish milieu. But there is no doubt that the distinctive characteristics of mysticism in these Jewish movements derived from an external source. Scholem made a decisive scholarly contribution towards the discovery of these very facts (see his book *On the Origins of Kabbalah*). But it is astonishing to see his effort to soften the impact of these factual determinations and to argue that, beyond these facts, there is some internal continuity of mysticism within Judaism and its sources. Especially characteristic in this regard are his assertions in the essay "Jewish Esoterica and the *Kabbalah*." See *Explications and Implications*, pp. 231-2.

55 The discussion of this issue has recently been summarized by Benjamin Oppenheimer in his article "Biblical Theology and Monotheistic Myth," *Immanuel*, No. 14 (1982), pp. 7-26.

There are those who claim that the belief in uniqueness, as formulated in the prophetic teaching, developed through a process of de-mythologization. This demythologization is seen as the counter-response to the polytheistic religions which were mythological by nature. There are also those who claim that the belief in uniqueness generated an original distinctive myth for the religion of Israel, and that this myth differed from those of the surrounding polytheistic religions. Scholem alludes to this debate in one of his articles.[56] In that essay, he seems to agree with the first of the two viewpoints. That is to say, he believes that there is a tendency toward demythologization in the thought of the prophets, but this tendency remained limited to a small circle of the spiritual elite and was not allowed to disseminate among the people. According to this same article, one can discern a continuation of the demythologizing tendency in post-biblical religious thought. Scholem sees this tendency reaching its peak in medieval Jewish philosophy, especially in the religious philosophy of Maimonides.

On the other hand, Scholem also posits that together with the trend toward myth-destruction there was a simultaneous development of a quite different trend that can be traced back to the biblical era. In spite of the prophets' castigations, there was a popular tendency to hold onto various myths since the people could not deal with an "abstract" divinity. The people needed to experience the presence of a living divinity. It follows that the *Kabbalah* represents a continuation of this popular trend. Moreover, says Scholem, this trend served as a foothold for authentic Jewish mysticism. It is worth noting that Scholem's argument depicts popular religion as the foothold for a religious development which, in later periods, became the strictly guarded esoteric property of a small elite.

Admittedly, in this article, Scholem expresses his views very briefly and with a generality that is uncharacteristic of his scholarly writings. In any case, if we have correctly understood the basic assumption underlying his argument in this article, it is doubtful

56 See the essay *"Kabbalah* and Myth" in *On the Kabbalah and Its Symbolism*, pp. 87-89.

that his position can withstand exacting criticism. Can the God of the prophets in fact be defined as an "abstract divinity"? Did the prophets not stand before a "living God," a creator and leader who commands and judges, exhibits pity and rage, rewards virtue and harkens to prayer? Is it indeed the case that only a god who has a mythological image can provide his believers with the experience of real presence? Is it true that only such an experience can sustain a popular religion?

The scholarly literature seems to point to a much more complex reality than that suggested by Scholem. There is indeed a basis for the theory which points to demythologization in the worldview of the prophets, but this demythologyzing process applies only to depictions of divine revelation and to distinctly polytheistic myths. This does not imply that the god of the prophets was perceived as an "abstraction." By refraining from describing God's image mythologically and from "deciphering" the secrets of his "nature" one does not negate an intense experience of personal presence which radiates with the believer's moral pathos and absolute intention of will. Through his concealed essence, the god of the prophets acts directly upon human beings. Human beings sense God's relation to them. They feel his love, grace, and compassion, as well as his zeal and wrath.

Thus, while the prophets may have rejected polytheistic myths and refrained from direct descriptions of God's image, this does not mean that they refrained from creating a different myth. This alternative myth differed from the polytheistic one not only in its "narrative plot," but also with respect to its experiential content, which comprised the raw material for mythological formulation. It also differed in the character of the mythic formulation itself. We are referring, of course, to the historical myth that describes the drama of God's leadership among his people.[57] It encompasses the

57 It is worth noting in passing that the first person to deal with the special character of the Jewish myth and to characterize this myth as one which molds historical themes, as opposed to the pagan myth which shapes themes from the life of nature, was one of the notable representatives of reform theology, Samuel Hirsch. See his systematic work, *Die Religionis Philosophie der Juden* (Leipzig: n.p., 1842). Cf. Eliezer Schweid, *The History of Jewish Thought in the Modern Era*, in Hebrew, Ch. VII.

stories of creation, the patriarchs, the exodus from Egypt, the revelation of *Torah,* the wanderings in the desert, the settlement in the land of Israel, the monarchy and the establishment of the temple, their destruction, and the vision of the coming redemption. Later on these were supplemented with the story of the return to Zion and the vision of the final redemption.

Once more, we must note that in this historical myth God appears before his people and its chosen individuals as creator, ordainer, leader and redeemer. God's presence is not an abstraction. It can be felt in history even when God conceals his face from his people and abandons them to their fate as a punishment. That is to say, although the prophetic myth neither formulates God's image nor deciphers his nature, it does express in a very tangible way his presence and the deliberate relation which he directs personally toward his People and its select individuals. Therefore, it is not the absence of myth in the prophetic teaching that places the prophets' "religion" beyond the pale of mysticism. Rather, it is actually the presence of a different myth which is neither mystical nor, to begin with, capable of comprising a matrix for mysticism — even after ever-deepening crises resulting from the "concealment of God's visage." For it should be emphasized that man's crisis when divinity hides forms an integral part of the historical myth itself. The ethical-emotional character of the relation between God and his people defines the state of divine hiddenness as an inevitable possibility. The realization of this possibility is unavoidable because of man's character and the essential status pertaining to man. For this reason, mysticism is not the anticipated response to crisis. Rather, as noted above, the anticipated response is atonement.

Even when it was first created, the historical myth set forth by the prophets was not the foundation for the religion of a select few who were elevated above the people. It was designed to be the foundation of a popular religion. And indeed this is precisely what the myth has become, at least since the period following the babylonian exile. No process of demythologization, not even that

73

expressed in the most radical philosophical interpretation of Maimonides, could damage and suppress the myth. Moreover, it is through this myth — and this myth alone — that the popular Jewish religion was continuously sustained from one generation to the next!

In fact, the historical myth created by the prophets did not overcome the entire legacy of polytheistic myths which Israelite religion absorbed from its cultural surroundings. The bible contains fragments of myths describing the appearance of God in creation and prophecy, and there are polytheistic elements in the biblical ritual. This surely attests to the suggestive power of these elements.[58] So it appears that the historical myth did not satisfy a particular type of worshipper. These worshippers retained polytheistic elements within the context of a general commitment to the teachings of the prophets. But there remains a bitter tension between these elements and the views of the prophets. This poses a serious difficulty for later interpreters of Scripture.

In any case, it appears that the prophetic teaching tolerated, from within, a certain "baggage" of religious views and tendencies that do not blend consistently with the prophetic doctrines. A scientific account of Judaism's history must also take account of this fact and note its vital significance.[59] Like all historical religions, the Israelite religion was never "pure." Moreover, the presence of polytheistic mythological elements in the original authoritative source, the Bible, provided a foothold for myths from the polytheistic environment during later periods.

Thus, if one wishes, one may say that the presence of alien myths from the cultural environment of the Israelite people represents a vital, or even a necessary component in the Israelite religion's historical character. "Judaism" also constituted the totality of influences it absorbed from its surroundings. The fact is that

58 See footnote 52. This refers to stories such as the descent of the sons of the gods in Genesis, and the hints found in the Book of Job about God's war against the powers of nature.
59 These claims depend especially upon Yehezkel Kaufmann's discussion in *The Religion of Israel*, Books II and III.

Judaism was able to absorb and tolerate such elements, albeit only under certain conditions and in limited amounts. This certainty points to one of Judaism's essential characteristics. It is the religion of an entire people seeking to live as a people and to settle as a people, even in a diasporic environment that limited the possibilities for cultural creativity.

So it was incumbent upon Judaism to confront the religions governing its host cultures. Judaism also had to adapt itself to these cultures, and the dialectical process of confrontation and adaptation created a unique spiritual apparatus within the Jewish religion in the areas of myth, theology, and *halakhah*. Studying Jewish mysticism may greatly help our understanding of Judaism's development and of the network interconnecting the Jewish religion and the cultures which the Jewish people confronted. But this contribution is mainly significant for understanding the nature and the *modus operandi* of the aforementioned spiritual apparatus. At times, this apparatus was able to integrate even the most alien and distant elements and to transform them into components of the thematic cycle which supported the Jewish people's emotions, worldview, and way of life.

Scholem's studies form part of the extensive scholarly data confirming this point. Its first proponent is R. Nahman Krochmal in his book, *Guide for the Perplexed of Our Time*.[60] Those who argue for the distinctively heterogeneous character of Judaism as a religious culture can substantiate their argument by pointing to significant influences deriving from the Babylonian, Egyptian, Canaanite, Persian, Greek and Roman cultures, as well as to the later influences of cultures shaped by Christianity and Islam.

The prophets and sages of Israel were engaged in intense conflicts with these cultures and religions. But, at the same time, they were ensnared by the magic of these cultures and religions. They

---

60 This is the conception which unifies R. Nahman Krochmal's views on the history of the people of Israel and its status among the nations. But Krochmal also applied this concept in chapters devoted to historical research; see Ch. 15 of *Guide for the Perplexed of Our Time*, in Hebrew, which is devoted to "external paths."

endeavored to decipher the secret of this magic from within the depths of their own religious creations.

To be sure, an essential matter finds expression in the believer's insistence on portraying elements absorbed from the outside as internal developments. This attests to the Jews' strong desire to preserve a line of continuity and a principle of purity. But scholars who adopt the tools of historical research will usually find little difficulty in identifying the external source and uncovering the channels of influence. It thus seems that the truly significant point concerning these influences is that they reveal an indefatigable effort to internalize the influences of an external culture and to incorporate them as integral parts of religious life. If it is psychologically correct to assert that the internalization of the 'not me' is essential to the dialectical process through which a personality develops, then Scholem is right to argue that the historical development of Judaism would be inconceivable without mysticism. Yet equally, Judaism's development would be inconceivable without philosophy and, generally speaking, without the tension arising from its own dependence upon alien elements — even upon elements that represent its diametrical opposite.

That is, the mysticism we find in Judaism during the post-biblical period does not flow from the internal development of the unique biblical faith. Rather, it expresses the dialectical relation of religious Jews to instances of 'the other,' 'the alien' and 'the opposite' which had crossed their path. Influences from shifting cultural environments were absorbed through a very long process. This explains the great variation of movements that emerged among the Jewish people over the course of its history. The richness accumulates, and the multi-layered baggage of the past comprises a foothold for far-reaching innovations. Through a selective use of sources, these innovations are endowed with the authority of a revelation generated from within. But what is truly amazing is that, despite this lengthy accumulation, the continuous tradition of truly substantial elements in the unique biblical faith was neither severed nor obscured. Despite the great variation one discerns that these elements are set apart as a distinct realm even in the creations of full-fledged mystics and philosophers who strive to integrate their religious world.[61]

Scholem's voluminous scholarly research surely demonstrated the rich multifacetedness of Jewish religious culture. Judaism, claimed Scholem — and we shall return to this claim later on — is not susceptible to a single dogmatic characterization. It is multifaceted and wrought with contradiction and vicissitude. The history of Jewish mysticism demonstrates this point in one generation after the next. But perhaps, precisely because this assertion is correct, these mystical movements should not be seen as the secret of Judaism's unity and continuity. Furthermore, perhaps we should not say that these movements embody Judaism's ability to overcome severe crises and to renew itself.

Mystical movements appeared, for the most part, as a secondary supportive crutch which was vital for specific parties within the people. During certain periods, these mystical movements became rather important for the rabbinic leadership, since it was the leaders, not the larger masses of Jewish householders, who carried the burden of struggling with external influences. Furthermore, the rabbinic leaders had to cope with elites who became so ensnared by external influences that there was a danger of their leaving the pale of the Jewish community.[62] But there was a catastrophic avalanche each time these mystical movements

61 Scholem also notes that for the most part, men of *halakhah* who were also Kabbalists preserved a clear demarcation between their work in *halakhah* and their work in *Kabbalah*. But we also refer to the fact that in conjunction with their esoteric mystical creations, the Kabbalists themselves produced an intellectual and educational creation which is not mystical, and which does not depend on mysticism for its application. In this regard, the most interesting example is Nahmanides, who was a Kabbalist and who also hinted at the fact that he was privy to secrets attained through *Kabbalah*. But his published works, including his interpretation of the *Torah*, are not Kabbalistic. In his work, he responds to the spiritual needs of his contemporaries without appealing to mysticism and without sacrificing his deep reflexive dimension.

62 We refer especially to the role fulfilled by *Kabbalah* within the world of scholarly sages (*talmidei hakhamim*) in the thirteenth century. The intellectual elite relied upon Maimonides, while the rabbinic intellectual elite relied upon *Kabbalah* for a deep dimension in its struggle against tendencies that emerged among the intellectual elite. See Fritz Baer, *The History of the Jews in Christian Spain*, in Hebrew, Part I, Ch. III, section IV.

deviated from their role as secondary support. These debacles were inherent whenever mystical movements gravitated toward the center of religious experience to replace what is termed "normative Judaism" together with its distinctive myth and injunctions. At these junctures, the responsible Jewish leadership responded by taking strong exception to mysticism and by returning to the life of *Torah* and divine injunctions in their "plain sense."[63]

ii. Unity and Continuity in Jewish History

We must now study closely Scholem's repeated claim that Judaism is not unitary and cannot simply be defined as a worldview, a religious experience, or even a way of life. Judaism is the totality of spiritual creations produced within the Jewish people's sphere of life. As such, Judaism is heterogeneous. It encompasses movements that contradict one another in their beliefs, viewpoints, and ways of life. Scholem's emphasis on the point is related to the context of an actual debate which took place during his day. In this controversy, Scholem was representing a typical nationalist-zionist perspective. According to this perspective, one should not set a preconceived limit to what can be encompassed within the concept "Judaism." Furthermore, no spiritual creation should be disqualified a priori as an "alien element" unworthy of dissemination among the Jewish masses.[64]

Mysticism, which embodies many diverse trends and manifests a great measure of Zionism's own revolutionary boldness, bestows historical legitimacy upon revolutionary boldness. From this position, Scholem sought to undermine the dogmatic theological definitions of the *Wissenschaft des Judentums* and of idealistic

63 We are referring to the responses of famous sages such as R. Nissim Gerundi, R. Isaac Ben-Sheshet, and R. Hasdai ben Abraham Crescas. These three took exception to both philosophy and *Kabbalah*. They attempted to develop a theology which absorbs the influence of *Kabbalah* and philosophy, but which teaches simple fear of God through the study of *Torah* and the fulfillment of *Mitzvot*. See Eliezer Schweid, *The Religious Philosophy of R. Hasdai ben Abraham Crescas*, in Hebrew (Jerusalem: Makor, 1971), Ch. II, III.
64 The clearest and most striking formulation of this view is found in the context of Scholem's discussion of the status of faith among the Sabbatians.

78

nineteenth-century Jewish philosophy. In addition, he sought to undermine Orthodox Judaism's definition of orthopraxis. Speaking rather hyperbolically, one may say that in at least several of Scholem's essays, revolutionary change is defined as more legitimately Jewish than all those approaches anchored in halakhic or dogmatic discipline.

In fact, although these views are sharply formulated in several of Scholem's essays, they do not exhaust his approaches to the subject. Through his characteristic manner of paradoxical dialectics, Scholem makes several statements which seem to contradict these views directly. First of all, while Scholem may have shattered Judaism's claim to unity by revealing mysticism as a perpetual revolution, it is noteworthy that at the same time, he maintained as one of his major aims in studying mysticism to decipher the

Perhaps it is even unnecessary to look for specific Christian influences where the respective situations are so similar. Early Sabbatianism and the early church went similar ways in accordance with the same psychological laws. But however that may be, the fact remains that at the very beginning of the movement pure faith, independent of the observance of the Law, was proclaimed as the supreme religious value, which secured salvation and eternal life for the believers. We should note in passing that this proclamation did not provoke the reaction one would have expected if some of today's cliches regarding the "essence" of Judaism and Christianity were correct. As a matter of fact, they are not, and most generalizations on the subject of Jewish versus Christian religiosity are more than doubtful. There is no way of telling *a priori* what beliefs are possible or impossible within the framework of Judaism. Certainly no serious historian would accept the specious argument that the criteria of "Jewish" belief were clear and evident until the *Kabbalah* beclouded and confused the mind. The Jewishness in the religiosity of any particular period is not measured by dogmatic criteria that are unrelated to actual historical circumstances, but solely by what sincere Jews do, in fact, believe, or — at least consider to be legitimate possibilities. There was no general and immediate rabbinical outcry against the Sabbatian definition of the "holy faith" (as it was called as early as 1666). Many rabbis adopted the "faith," and there were few who opposed it only on grounds of principle. Extreme caution should, therefore, be exercised before pronouncing on the "Jewish" (namely, "un-Jewish") character of spiritual phenomena in Jewish history.

Sabbatai Sevi, pp. 283-4

These are sharp and piercing comments. But nevertheless, in typical fashion, despite this sharp, vigorous and principled formulation which denies any preconceived historical-philosophical or dogmatic definition of the essence of Judaism, Scholem himself returns to the issue of the contrast between Sabbatianism and Christianity (*Sabbatai Sevi*, pp. 795-800). This time, he makes statements which come very close to this same type of a priori historical-philosophical definition. Needless to say, such a definition is also employed in the discussions mentioned above.

secret of Judaism's unity and continuity as a cultural-religious phenomenon.

Clearly, Scholem regarded mysticism as the secret key to the interiority and unity of Judaism throughout the generations — if only by virtue of its revolutionary boldness. Within mysticism all the contradictions emerge. Nonetheless, in mysticism, the roots of these contradictions also merge into a unity. But beyond Scholem's dialectical use of mystical piety's categories, we also find the scholar continually wondering what characterizes Jewish mysticism as a distinctly Jewish phenomenon? Scholem ends up presupposing, as a matter of course, that there are distinctively Jewish characteristics in any mysticism that can be defined as Jewish. He believes that these characteristics can be discerned clearly, and determined a priori. Moreover, as we saw above, he does not hesitate to point out some of these characteristics explicitly.

A typical case in point is the argument in Scholem's article "Meditations On The Possibility Of Jewish Mysticism In Our Day."[65] In this essay, Scholem claims that a particular type of mysticism (that which strives for a unification of the human spirit with divine substance) is inconceivable within Judaism. No less typical is his claim that a religious movement cannot be called Jewish if it does not maintain a belief in "Torah from heaven" in the fundamental sense. This argument returns us directly to the bosom of orthodoxy. Similarly, in the essay on "Kabbalah and Myth" one discovers that in Scholem's view, the original essence of Judaism was "ethical monotheism."[66] Consequently, limitations and qualifications were imposed on any mysticism within the realm of Judaism. Unfortunately, this claim returns Scholem directly to the idealistic Jewish philosophy of the nineteenth century. We cannot regard these comments as incidental and exceptional, for with them as base, Scholem defined the distinctive elements of Jewish mysticism in the methodological discussion

---

65 See "Reflections on the Possibility of Jewish Mysticism in Our Day," *Explications and Implications,* pp. 71-83.
66 Appears in *On the Kabbalah and Its Symbolism.*

beginning his book *Major Trends*.[67] Furthermore, in the article "Reflections on Jewish Theology," Scholem posits these remarks as a basis for his explicitly a priori determination that rejection of certain assumptions entails exclusion from Judaism.[68]

We mentioned above how these seemingly contradictory statements may be reconcilable within a dialectical outlook. But it is also worth stating that Scholem himself did not see the need to point out the dialectical tension between his contradictory claims. Furthermore, he did not attempt to reconcile these claims within the framework of a comprehensive and systematic view of Judaism. For purportedly good reasons (which he kept to himself) he dismissed such attempts quite adamantly, out of hand. The trouble is that such an attempt is called for by the internal logic of Scholem's own statements. In his the essay "Reflections on Jewish Theology," he nearly concedes this need, although he does not see the possibility of addressing it.

We thus find ourselves facing contradictory assertions that we cannot reconcile without assuming that Judaism has clear and distinctive characteristics in the realms of belief, opinion, symbols, ordinances and historical myth. These characteristics all derive from Scripture, and they are also clearly discernible in later stages of Judaism's development. However their existence did not preclude Judaism's wide and varied relationships with other religions and cultures. External influences were confronted alternatively through the paths of resistance and integration.

These confrontations generated abundant and contradictory religious movements within the Jewish people's sphere of life. That is to say, to begin with there was unity, or at least an authoritative claim to unity. *Ex post facto,* there was plurality. This bestows some legitimacy upon both the historian who claims to discover the plurality, and upon the theologian who points to the thread of continuity and its authoritative claim. There will be no

---

67 See also the second section of the essay "Kabbalah And Myth" in *On the Kabbalah and Its Symbolism.*
68 *Explications and Implications,* pp. 537-556; cf. *Ariel,* No.2 (1973).

contradiction between the original demand and the ultimate result if one carefully guards the line of demarcation between the substantial core of the Jewish religion and the elements generated through its connection with what is 'other' and 'alien.'

Although this argument takes exception to Scholem's views, it may actually be supported by his scholarly works. From Scholem's research, we learn that the argument which rejects out of hand any a priori definition of Judaism was based on a hastily formed judgement that ultimately had to be refuted. This argument transcended the limits imposed by the expectations of Scholem himself, who sought to contribute to the continuity of Judaism. It also transcended the limits of Scholem's scholarly findings. If Scholem had chosen to offer a comprehensive historical account of Judaism from the biblical period up to our time, rather than to focus his view on one of its streams, his books would not create the impression that this "mystical" stream incorporates, through its very plurality, the historical backbone of the Jewish religion. As a matter of course, he also would also have been unable to reject in such an absolute and blatant fashion some of the systematic determinations posited by the scholars of *Wissenschaft des Judentums* and by the Jewish theologians of the nineteenth and twentieth centuries. In the early stages of his career, Scholem dismissed these determinations in rapid succession. Yet ultimately he himself relied on the very same assertions. He appealed to them when they allowed him to imply his own solution to Judaism's spiritual problems in our time.

iii. Christianity and Sabbatianism

In the preceding discussion, we noted the dialetic of differentiation and attachment between those themes which distinguish the Jewish religion and those which the Jewish religion absorbed from its cultural environment. The inherently problematic nature of this dialectic was revealed most starkly and bitterly in those historical cases of mystical movements originating in Judaism which ultimately broke completely with the Jewish people's continuous historical existence as a people defined within its own framework. Scholem himself examined two such cases, Christianity in the ancient period, and Sabbatianism, a movement which straddled the border between the middle ages and modernity.[69]

The first case concerns a mystical movement generated within the Jewish people and anchored in Judaism's sources. But this movement was severed from Judaism when it chose to adhere to the messianic myth while discarding from this myth both the *halakhah* and those religious themes expressed in a way of life governed by the fulfillment of halakhic ordinances. Early Christianity established itself as a new religion that conveyed its message to peoples who had previously worshipped polytheistic gods.

The scholarly study of this movement demands a comparison between Judaism and Christianity that aims to discern the differential characteristics separating these two religions and to distinguish each of them in their own right. This comparison is necessary despite Scholem's claim that it is impossible to determine decisively whether a certain characteristic or view is "possible" in Christianity and "impossible" in Judaism. More than once or twice, Scholem himself violated this constraint which he imposed upon others. Obviously, neither Judaism nor Christianity was a historically "pure" religions. Over the the long period during which these religions co-existed in close proximity and engaged in perpetual conflict, each absorbed influences from the other. We thus find Christian characteristics in Jewish religious movements and vice versa. It is further obvious that when speaking of two religions that were so actively connected with one another, it is impossible to distinguish with certainty between developments generated by the influence of other religions, and those originating in a dialectic of response to the challenges posed by identical historical circumstances. But in spite of all these qualifications, one cannot avoid a typological comparison that characterizes each of

69 The statements on Christianity appear in Scholem's book on Sabbatai Sevi, especially in Ch. I and VI.

these two religions according to its own essential viewpoints, symbols, and modes of worship.

In the previous discussion, we described the Jewish religion as one which, even in its innocent stage, was reflexive and conscious of the crisis perpetually lurking at its doorstep. We also noted that the responses which overcame this crisis, insofar as they were generated by the religion's primal-original framework, followed the route of atonement rather than that of mysticism. By contrast, the Christian religion was originally a mystical religious movement even before it separated from Judaism. When it severed itself from Judaism, Christianity decisively rejected Judaism's non-mystical elements. Early Christianity thus established itself as a mystical movement during its primal and "innocent" stage. One may perhaps demonstrate that some of early Christianity's mystical themes are found in previous mystical movements that arose among the Jewish people, but even so, it clearly changes in a revolutionary way the relation between the primary and secondary elements in Judaism. Indeed, what placed Christianity beyond the pale of Judaism was the establishment of these mystical elements as a central Christian tenet and as a content in the manifest gospel Christianity directed to the popular classes embracing it. This clearly marks a typological distinction between the Jewish religion, which is essentially non-mystical, and other religions which are fundamentally and essentially mystical.

The second case mentioned above, Sabbatianism, once again involves a mystical movement that developed within the Jewish people's sphere of life. But the Sabbatian movement did not succeed in sustaining itself outside of this sphere. Indeed, its failure as a messianic-mystical project led Sabbatianism to turn against all the substantial elements of "normative" Judaism. For this reason, the movement was vomited up and ejected from the Jewish people's recognized sphere of life. Insofar as this movement continued to exist, it proclaimed the redemption of the Jewish people by means of their own destruction. In other words, the movement perceived of the Jewish people's destruction as its redemption.

84

What caused this frightening distortion if not, once again, the establishment of the mystical element as a tenet of faith and a constituent of the message directed toward the popular classes embracing Sabbatianism? Did these processes not extend so far as to sever Sabbatianism from the traditional Jewish religion of *Torah* and divine ordinances?

The saga of these two movements' development and fate conveys a sufficiently clear historical lesson. For individuals, mysticism can be the essence of their religious experience. But when mysticism bursts from the periphery and directs itself to the center of mass religion, and when it breaks from the limiting constraints imposed by the historical myth and divine ordinances of Judaism, it either abandons the Jewish people's sphere of life or turns to destroy this sphere from within. Consequently, it is absurd to describe either Christianity or Sabbatianism as a "continuation" of Judaism, even if one adopts a dialectical-paradoxical orientation.[70] It is indeed possible that each living religion tolerates internal paradoxes — co-exists with them through dialectical means — but no spiritual movement can tolerate paradoxes that damage its essential core.

In studies devoted to Sabbatianism, Scholem sought to demonstrate that even this movement can be seen, through a dialectic, as a continuation fertilizing the spiritual products of the Jewish religion.[71] Later on, we will have to return to this issue for a more detailed discussion. At present, it suffices to say that this argument is implausible. Perhaps a few of the Hassids and the adherents of the Jewish enlightenment *(Maskilim)* emerged from Sabbatian circles or had some encounters with Sabbatians. But nonetheless, these people had to overcome their Sabbatian background,

70 See Baruch Kurzweil's critique in "Notes On Gershom Scholem's *Sabbatai Sevi*" in *The Struggle Over the Values of Judaism*, Hebrew (Jerusalem: Shocken, 1970), pp. 99ff.
71 This requires a clarification, like the point stated in footnote 46. Scholem noted and even emphasized the destructive character of Sabbatianism. He also claimed that Sabbatianism reached a total impasse (see *Sabbatai Sevi*, Ch. VII). What we have here is a "dialectical" relationship which, more than once, is almost paradoxical. It is quite difficult to reconcile such paradoxes within the context of a unified worldview. Nevertheless, this is quite typical of Scholem's thought.

uprooting it totally from their hearts, in order to find their way to Hassidim or to the Jewish enlightenment. As far as they were concerned, Sabbatianism as a spiritual movement could only symbolize a dangerous border, for those who trespassed this boundary would seldom return. Only those who managed to return to the previous layers and re-attach themselves to non-mystical elements of normative Judaism were able to regain their moorings in Judaism and to suggest paths for its continuity.

CHAPTER 5

MYSTICISM IN RABBINIC JUDAISM

i. Normative and Popular Judaism

The borderline cases mentioned above shed light on the place of mystical movements within rabbinic Judaism. We have already noted that although several prominent Jewish sages were mystics, it does not mean that in their manifest functions in the realms of *aggadah* and *halakhah* they projected mystical thinking onto beliefs, opinions and modes of behavior disseminated among the people. Scholem determines decisively that until the aftermath of the Spanish expulsion, mysticism was an esoteric movement quite wary of disseminating its ways and views to the public. Consequently, mysticism antedating the expulsion from Spain must be seen as a kind of internal support for a small elite, even though the exoteric creations of this elite may have occupied an authoritative status.

Ostensibly, Scholem's own testimony implies this conclusion. But such a conclusion cannot be reconciled with his general supposition that mysticism is the core rejuvenating Judaism, enabling it to overcome its crises and to renew itself from one generation to the next.

Indeed, we now stand before another issue enveloped in a thick fog. We refer to Scholem's claim that mysticism also exerted some influence upon the "popular religion" of Israel, not only after the expulsion from Spain, but during earlier periods as well.[72] How

---

72 The difficulties inherent in this aspect of Scholem's thought are concentrated in one passage that appears in the introduction of his essay "Jewish Esoterica and *Kabbalah*." This passage is worth quoting in its entirety.

If we summarize the development of Jewish mysticism from a historical perspective, we must say that its special character and the principal message of its development inhere in the fact that we are dealing with mystical movements that progressively strive to increase their social and national influence. During the first period, this tendency will not yet be discerned. In the second and third periods, this tendency already reveals itself with various degrees of clarity. But in these three periods, the tendency is revealed through a sharp dialectic. Thus, we have here a distinct and unique development that is in accord with those internal laws which determine the course of the Jewish religion's

are we to comprehend this claim? In what way could an esoteric movement exert such a decisive influence upon something referred to as "popular religion"? Does Scholem mean to suggest a sharp distinction between what is called "rabbinic Judaism" or "normative Judaism" (which is of course the "institutionalized" religion),

history. On the other hand, it is clear that in all periods of the Jewish religion's history, one also discerns the influences of the surrounding environment and of the general contemporaneous trends in the non-Jewish world. These two influences are not always equal in measure. However, Jewish historiography in general, and that of the nineteenth century in particular, erred in emphasizing the external influences. The truth is that Jewish Esoterica (*Ha-mistorin Hayehudi*) in each and every era undoubtedly contained a distinctive Jewish profile, despite external influences. Moreover, among the religious trends in Judaism after the destruction of the Jewish Temple, *Kabbalah* was the current that succeeded, through religious prodding, in exercising a deep spiritual influence upon the multitudes, and it also had the capacity to gain control over these people. This development must be explained in relation to the distinctive character of medieval Jewish mysticism. In this case, mysticism stands in competition with the trends revealed especially in rationalistic Jewish philosophy of the twelfth and thirteenth centuries. Both the movement of philosophizing intellectuals and that of Kabbalists, bearers of secrets and mystery, had an aristocratic character. These men appear with the explicit intention of teaching their doctrines to only a few select individuals who are especially deserving. But the sources for the sustenance of *Kabbalah* run deep within the roots of the popular religion, and as long as *Kabbalah* was truly a vital religious force, we find it in a vigorous relationship with the national myth and with the religion of the simple Jew. And thus, another paradox emerges; the Kabbalists appear as representatives of those religious forces and beliefs which were active among the masses, even though these forces and beliefs are expressed in a language of religious ideology and frequently even in the philosophers' mode of thought and speech. But in contrast to the philosophers' rationalism, the *Kabbalah's* mode of thought is determined by picturesque mythical thinking, and this is precisely what links it with the masses — more so than is readily apparent, if one judges only by its external appearances and its mode of thought, which are often quite strange and complex. In this movement, myth and mystery stand in a relationship of interdependence and reciprocal influence. This myth was combated, suppressed, or at any rate, banished to a peripheral position, by the classical forms and expression of the Jewish religion. But often the myth erupted with enormous force from the various forms of mystical thought and revealed itself as a power which in the past, and still today, maintains a sturdy and potent position in Judaism. And indeed, in this same respect, it is especially interesting to note the many Kabbalists who attempt to combine a mode of thought that is mythical and at times primitive with Judaism's strict monotheism. During various periods in the history of Jewish mysticism, and especially after the expulsion from Spain, these attempts led to a most important result: the *Kabbalah* was revealed as a force that, in its own way, brings about a revolution in Jewish consciousness. It is true that in the thinking of the Kabbalists themselves, the new and the old merge together well. They often saw themselves as the traditional and conservative representatives of ancient religious authority, while in truth, their activities tended to have precisely the opposite effect. When even the Kabbalists realize that their ideas are revolutionary with respect to rabbinic Judaism, they reach the verge of the mystical "heresy" and they find themselves on the verge of becoming entangled in

and the uninstitutionalized popular religion that managed to absorb mystical influences through its own esoteric means?

The subtle reader of Scholem's writings will find many implications toward the aforementioned distinction between normative rabbinic Judaism and popular Jewish religion. This distinction is presupposed by the very use of these two terms in a manner that attributes to each its own distinctive meaning. In Scholem's writings, we also find the suggestion that popular religion was somehow receptive to mysticism's influence. He thus alludes to certain popular customs that are magical in character. He also notes that the halakhah takes exception to these customs while mysticism provides an ideological background for them.[73] A more substantial allusion to this distinction appears in Scholem's treatment of messianic movements. These movements, which were instilled with apocalyptic fervor, surfaced time and again from the people's midst.[74]

In Scholem's opinion, this represents the distinct influence of mystical "utopianism." He further believes that there is a perpetual tension between mystical utopianism and the constraining approach of the masters of *halakhah*. Having emphasized these suggestive allusions, we must also stress that we did not find in Scholem's writings a systematic and crystallized distinction

a conflict with the "official" Judaism of their time. This conflict was at times covert and at times manifest.

Explications and Implications, pp. 231-2

This passage offers a cross-section of some of Scholem's basic assumptions regarding Jewish mysticism and its role in the history of the Jewish religion. The reader of this passage uncovers some of the historical and philosophical difficulties that were not reconciled in his writings. How may one see an essentially esoteric and aristocratic movement as a movement that is popular in nature? How does the mystical myth relate to the "popular" Jewish myth? How do "popular" religiosity and "classical," or "rabbinic" religiosity relate to mystical religiosity? Scholem presents all of these terms without defining them clearly, as if the distinction between them is readily apparent. He then tries to use these terms and general concepts such as "dialectic" and "paradox" to resolve the tensions that emerge between his historical findings and his presuppositions regarding the essence of mysticism and its role in Judaism. But it is highly doubtful that he succeeds in this.

73 See "Jewish Esoterica and *Kabbalah*," *Explications and Implications*, p. 233.
74 *Ibid.* Cf. "Toward an Understanding of the Messianic Idea in Judaism," in *The Messianic Idea in Judaism*, pp. 1-36.

between the two terms "normative Judaism," and "popular Judaism." Furthermore, we did not find an explanation of the manner through which mysticism filters down, as it were, to a people located "below" the barrier of esotericism. Indeed we might say that some of Scholem's claims implicitly contradict such a distinction.

We have already mentioned one of these assertions, Scholem's description of what he regards as the dramatic turnabout following the expulsion from Spain, when the kabbalists burst through the barrier of esotericism and began to propagate their teachings among the masses.[75] This description seems to imply a certain shift, not only in the normative realm, but also in the spiritual-religious atmosphere of the entire people.

Another assertion that contradicts the aforementioned distinction is implicit in Scholem's emphatic insistence on the centrality of the attitude to oral tradition. Scholem maintains that without the tradition of oral *Torah,* beliefs and opinions could not have been transformed into a people's way of life. This seems to imply that the Toraitic tradition actually was the popular religion! Should Scholem's writings on this issue perhaps be interpreted differently?

In any case, we seem to be dealing with a substantive difficulty that Scholem preferred to leave untouched. Yet, as we noted above, he did not refrain from using terms that alternately suggest the contrast and the similarity between popular and normative religion. Indeed, up to a point, such equivocal terminology is legitimate, inasmuch as Scholem is adhering to the dialectical tension within the tradition. But once one begins to discuss the issue of the relation between mysticism and the Jewish religion, it becomes impossible to justify evading of a systematic methodological account. In examining the universe of beliefs, opinions, customs and creations of Jewish communities in shifting places and times, one always discerns baggage of popular culture that is not part of the normative network striving to unify the Jewish

75 See *Sabbatai Sevi,* Ch. I.

people. Moreover, more than once or twice, the popular culture became loaded with elements to which the halakhic authorities objected. In these cases the authorities would try, not always with success, to remove and uproot this baggage from the people's midst.[76]

Nevertheless, it seems that any attempt among the Jewish people to distinguish systematically between two clearly demarcated categories of normative and popular religion is destined to fail. For these two do not exist without one another. This is true not only as a matter of historical fact, but also by their very nature. Consequently, to sever one from the other is to destroy both. We are dealing here with a distinctive characteristic of the Israelite religion that stems from its biblical sources. For this is a religion which was neither established as a church nor intended to be established as a church. Rather, it was designed as a complete way of life for the people of Israel. A complete way of life for a people reflects continuous activity of various internal and external elements. To begin with, these elements could not be encompassed or controlled by the normative religious system. But what the system could do, and what it actually did do, was to design, to mold and to synthesize its creations so as to include those cultural themes which came into being through the vital continuity of a tradition.

Consequently, until the modern age, no overall tension developed between the religious tradition on the one hand and the people's tendencies and way of life on the other. In addition, there was a crystallized process through which fertile themes were constantly injected from the people to the tradition. The tradition was also creatively molded for the people's benefit. For this process, highly sensitive and flexible mechanisms of *halakhah* and pedagogy were developed. We will mention two of these mechan-

---

76 One of the distinct examples of this type of tension is Abraham ben David's objection to Maimonides concerning the issue of divine images. Abraham ben David did not take exception to the tenet of the incorporeality of God, but rather to the halakhic determination that those who believe in the corporeality of God, according to a simplistic understanding of the words of the prophets, are in the category of heretics. This, therefore, is an expression of "tolerance" toward a view that was spreading among the people.

isms in general terms. First, the status accorded in the realm of *halakhah* to the people's customs. Second, the relative tolerance toward different beliefs and viewpoints within the realm of *aggadah*, as compared with the stability of the practically binding *halakhah*. In most periods and localities the normative religion of the people of Israel was spared by these mechanisms from institutional petrification and from the creation of a demarcating partition between (a) the beliefs and way of life prevailing among the majority of the people, and (b) the beliefs and customs of the leading religious elite. Judaism remained a popular religion that oriented itself toward the leading elite.

For this reason, it would be more precise to forego expressions such as the "normative religion" and the "popular religion" of the people of Israel. For the normative religion is also the popular religion. Instead of using two mutually exclusive terms misleadingly, it would be better to establish terms that indicate the internal tension between the normative elements and the popular elements of a Jewish religion which is unitary but which tolerates within it a rather substantial extent of heterogeneity. For the purpose of research and sequential analysis, it is both possible and necessary to distinguish between these different elements. But then, we must also consider a process that unifies them and that blends them into a dynamic unified tradition which transcends its multiple expressions in *aggadah* and *halakhah*.

These assertions also apply to the phenomena which Scholem saw as evidence of mysticism's influence upon popular Judaism. Even magical beliefs and practices — indeed even apocalyptic messianism — did not have to reach the people by esoteric routes from the beliefs of mystics who guarded the secrecy of their teachings. Popular magic had manifest channels of dissemination both in internal traditions passed from one generation to the next and also in external popular cultures surrounding the Jewish communities in every generation.

Likewise, apocalyptic messianism, which calculates and defers various culminations, did not need concealed mystical sources.

Apocalyptic messianism had its own source within the Jewish religion's overt myth of redemption. Already, during the biblical period, this myth was not entirely unitary. In fact, these same motifs of popular messianism are found in several chapters of the prophetic books, especially in Isaiah, Ezekiel, and Zachariah, as well as in several chapters of the *Ketubim* (Writings), especially in the book of Daniel. The midrashic literature that developed these motifs fitted, albeit as a heterogeneous component, with the overt myth of Judaism.

Indeed, one cannot deny that these motifs are receptive to mysticism. But in themselves, they do not fall within the category of mysticism. And just as they can be depicted as an indirect influence of mystical circles on popular religion, they can also be described as "footholds" in exoteric religious sources for the development of Jewish mysticism in esoteric circles. Moreover, one may indeed say that the existence of such "footholds" allows for a certain emanation of mystical thought from esoteric circles to wider circles among the people. Still, the aforementioned internal tensions within the Jewish religion are adequately explained by virtue of Judaism's inclusion of heterogeneous elements in its tradition. These elements derived from the need for a common cultural denominator with the environment, and from the fact that Judaism stood in perpetual conflict and perpetual cooperation with alien cultural environments.

In a word, the same characteristics that distinguished the religion of Israel during the biblical period also characterized the religion of Israel in the generations to come. Together with major changes, one also discerns a clear line of continuity through the sages' activities in the days of the second Temple, the Talmudic and Geonic periods, and the middle ages. Neither mysticism nor its indirect influence is the secret of this continuity. Rather, the secret is embodied in the manifest characteristics of popular "normative" Judaism which sought to shape the people's entire way of life.

ii. Law, Lore, and Liturgy

The Judaism that was crystallized by the early rabbinic sages (*hazal*) in their law and lore is a direct continuation, albeit with many changes in form, of the same themes that distinguished Israelite religion in the biblical period. Together with these old themes, there was a recurrent emergence, supplementation and accumulation of new themes. But the unifying center of gravity is clear enough.

The Judaism of the early rabbinic sages is a religion centering on the manifest way of life governed by study of *Torah* and the fulfillment of its ordinances. This way of life is based on the biblical myth that includes the stories of the creation, the patriarchs, the wanderings in the dessert, the settlement of the Land, the construction of the Temple, the monarchy, the decline, and the destruction. Historical continuity with the past was tied to an awareness of a new stage, requiring a more complex under-standing of the relation between the people and its God.[77] But there is a continuty of that historical framework which is oriented toward the goal of completing the myth in the messianic future. Above all, the way of life created on the basis of this myth succeeded in instilling the myth itself within the consciousness of the people. This was achieved through teaching and declamation as well as through prayer, recital of *Torah* and cultic ritual. The recollection of this myth established an experience of God's pres-ence among the people in the synagogues, the houses of learning, and the family home. This was not established through mysticism, but through the overt means of *"Torah* worship, and righteous deeds."[78]

These claims are not new. They are widely known, well-researched views which interpret what was said explicitly in the

77 This is attested to by the unceasing struggle with the question of the nature of the people of Israel's fate among the nations. On this issue, see Yehezkel Kaufmann, *The Religion of Israel*, in Hebrew, Vol. VIII, Book I (Jerusalem: Bialik-Devir Foundation, 1956).
78 *Mishnah Abot*, 1:2.

teachings of early rabbinic sages.[79] Our present concern is to re-establish that these views still capture the essence, despite the recent discovery of an affinity between many great Tannaitic figures and what scholars have called the "Jewish Gnosis." This discovery does indeed add another dimension to the works of early rabbinic sages. But it does not alter the image that the sages themselves wished to cast within the historical memory of their people. And by no means should one portray the mystical dimension alluded to in several aggadic and midrashic texts as the only, or even the major dimension to the early rabbinic sages' enterprise. On the contrary, the experiential-religious dimension contained in the manifest way of life and modes of worship is no less deep than the mystical element. Perhaps — this determination is admittedly a matter of personal taste — the former supercedes the latter. For the halakhic Judaism of the early rabbinic sages, including the *aggadic* dimension that accompanies their legal deliberations, is not to be seen merely as a normative institution. It constitutes a rich and complex part of the believer's life. In order to find the deep religious dimension which distinguishes this part of the believer's life, one must follow a path which differs from that of the mystic's heated explorations, but which nevertheless indicates the historical distinctiveness of Judaism.

A vast and diverse corpus of scholarly literature deals with the religious trends and way of life prevailing among the Jewish people during the mishnaic and talmudic periods. In recent times,

---

79 We will mention several works that are central to this problem:
   a. Isaac Heinemann, *Darkhei Ha-Aggadah*, in Hebrew (Jerusalem: Magnes, 1954).
   b. Ephraim Urbach, *Hazal: Pirkei Emunot Ve-Deot*, in Hebrew (Jerusalem: Magnes, 1969).
   c. Abraham Joshua Heschel, *Torah Min Hashamaim Ba-Aspaklariah Shel Ha-Dorot*, in Hebrew (London and New York: Shunzin, 1962).
   d. Solomon Schecter, *Aspects of Rabbinic Theology* (New York: Shocken, 1909).
   e. Avraham Holtz, *Be-Olam Hamahshavah Shel Hazal*, in Hebrew (Tel-Aviv: Sifriyat Ha-Poalim, 1979).

this corpus has expanded rapidly.[80] The discovery of fresh literary evidence casts new light upon the assumptions derived from the Oral *Torah* and from the sources known as "the external literature." Thus, we will be unable to formulate a balanced summary of these issues for some time to come. Today, scholars are naturally inclined to try to decipher themes that were overlooked by their predecessors. Indeed, contemporary scholars are uncovering, among other things, esoteric mystical trends operating on the periphery of the tannaitic circles or even within the world of the *Tannaim* themselves. These findings both verify and amplify Gershom Scholem's conclusions. The new data also overshadows the view prevailing among scholars of previous generations. Nevertheless, it seems that we should be wary of extreme interpretations of the picture that is taking shape before our eyes. Recent scholarship surely illustrates that during the period of the early sages, both the larger Jewish world and the world of the sages themselves was far more complex, wrought with contradiction, and infused with esoteric themes than was previously estimated by scholars basing their views primarily on the sources of the oral tradition (the Mishnah, the Talmuds, classical midrashic compilations, and the

80 The criticial-programmatic orientation of this work calls for a comprehensive argument. This comprehensiveness, in addition to the abundance, complexity and unsystematic quality of the literary material treated in this chapter, forces us to limit ourselves to a brief and general sketch. An elaborate discussion considering the rich corpus of scholarly research would demand an entire book. We will be able to speak a bit more extensively later on when we reach our discussion of medieval theology, which proposed various systematic approaches based on the writings of the early rabbinic sages. The preceding footnote presents some of the basic texts that influenced my account. For the purpose of establishing a contrast with new and critical approaches in the same areas, we mention the work of Professor Jacob Neusner, which is both original and impressive in its scope and its depth. As far as the present discussion is concerned, two of his works are especially noteworthy:

a. *Method and Meaning in Ancient Judaism*, Brown Judaic Studies, No. 10 (Chico, CA: Scholars Press, 1979). Readers of this volume will find a methodological and conceptual summary.

b. *Ancient Judaism: Debates and Disputes*, Brown Judaic Studies, No. 64 (Chico, CA: Scholars Press, 1984). This volume discusses a long series of new studies in the field we are examining.

The two works provide an extremely clear exposition of the difficulties arising in the scholarly study of mishnaic and talmudic Judaism. Despite significant differences in approach and emphasis, readers will find certain parallels between characteristics outlined in Neusner's works and the "standard patterns" emphasized in our discussion.

liturgical texts). Yet nevertheless, recent scholarship has not over-turned the overall portrait delineated by what anthropologists might call "the standard patterns" in the world of the sages.

These standard patterns reveal themselves not only in motifs that persist throughout generations of tradition, and throughout the bulk of oral *Torah* but also in the points of emphasis supported by the authority of toraitic pedagogy. These standard tendencies must be distinguished from the shifting attitudes of individual thinkers, even if such individuals were towering, influential figures. It is important and remarkably fascinating to ponder the diversity of opinions and religious experiences among prominent figures. But those who wish to describe the Jewish religion as a distinct historical phenomenon must transcend this diversity. It is necessary to examine what Jews universally accepted as the shared tradition entrusted to them and obligating all Jews throughout the generations. The following question must be addressed: in the estimation of the Jews, what doctrines must be preached, studied, and used for shaping both one's external way of life as well as the distinctive characteristics and experiences of the religious person? In order to answer this question, one must first examine the process of transmission that dictated the literary and pedagogical style of the Oral *Torah*. This process emphasized the study of *Torah* "for its own sake" as a central religious value. Secondly, one ought to examine the themes and forms of historical memory formulated in the realm of *halakhah* (law) and in the context of *aggadah* (lore) surrounding scriptural exegesis and the interpretation of festivals and appointed times for communal worship. Third, one should explore the religious ethos of the early rabbinic sages. In both its law and its lore, the rabbinic ethos affirms the centrality of divine commandments which rest on an acceptance of divine governance. Finally, one should examine the patterns and themes of public liturgy shaped by the early rabbinic sages. These forms of worship constituted the major expression of the Jewish person's sense of presence among his people and before his God. In all of these areas, one finds footholds for mystical interpretation and experience. Furthermore, the subsequent discussion suggests that these elements flow directly from distinctive features that characterized the Jewish religion in the biblical period.

The study of *Torah* for its own sake is a religious value. Such study in and of itself embodies a religious experience, the exploration and deep understanding of God's Word and his commandments. But there is no mysticism in this study. This much can be deduced from the focus on halakhic themes relating to all aspects of man's earthly life, and from the distinctly intellectual character of the pedagogical process exemplified in the Talmudic genre.[81] Through their halakhic norms (which generate symbols, festivals, appointed times, and days of commemoration) and through their aggadic interpretations of biblical stories, the early rabbinic sages repeatedly expounded themes drawn from a distinctive historical, narrative, and ritualistic memory. The memories conveyed through the rabbinic norms and interpretations form a direct continuation of the Bible's historical myth, which includes tales of the patriarchs, the bondage in Egypt, the exodus, the revelation of *Torah,* the sin of the golden calf, the wanderings in the desert, settlement of the land of Israel, construction of the Temple, the prosperity in the days of David and Solomon, the period of decline, the split between the kingdoms of Judaea and Israel, the subsequent destruction and exile, the return to Zion, and the recurrence of decay and destruction, as well as the anticipation of future redemption.

Once more, this myth conveys the notion of a people governed by God through the paths of history in accordance with the covenant sealed between God and his people, the covenant of *Torah*. This ancient myth gradually reaches a more profound confrontation with the problems of justice and divine providence,

---

81 A very clear definitive account of this matter can be found in E. Uhrbach's "The Religious Significance of Halakhah," in Hebrew, in his *Al Yahadut Vehinukh* (Jerusalem: Hebrew University Press, 1967), pp. 127-139.

which are the most basic problems for comprehending the distinctively moral relationship between the people and their God.[82]

The moral doctrines of the early rabbinic sages are not mystical. The sages' teaching focuses primarily upon a religious awe of God mediated through *halakhah* and the fulfillment of divine injunctions. Pursuit of virtue is achieved through discovering God's will in the *Torah,* which is passed on and interpreted throughout the generations. Finally, the public liturgy surely is not mystical. The essential elements of prayer are the centrality of the *Torah*-reading in synagogue, and the recital of the *Shema* and its blessings and of the eighteen benedictions. All of these elements, which together comprise the liturgical product of the early rabbinic sages, derive from the narratives, prophecies, and poetry of the bible. Since liturgy is especially important for our discussion of the Jew's experience of presence before God, let us expound this subject a bit further.[83]

What then are the themes which come to expression in the public liturgy instituted by the early rabbinic sages? A recollection of the historical events that founded the Jewish faith and reveal God's governance over his people. Among these events are the exodus from Egypt, the splitting of the Red Sea, and the revelation of *Torah.* The liturgy also generates a view of redemption that includes the reinstatement of the kingdom of Judaea and of the sacrifices in the Temple of Jerusalem. In addition the prayers remind the Jew that he is obliged to express love for God by fulfilling God's commandments and by contemplating divine *Torah.* These recollections place the Jew within the framework of his people's historical myth. In the next stage of the liturgy, the Jew stands in judgement before God, confesses his sins, requests forgiveness, and expresses his hope to be absolved and earn God's

82 This subject is treated extensively and in depth in J.H. Yerushalmi's book, *Zakhor: Jewish History and Jewish Memory* (Seattle and London: University of Washington Press, 1982).
83 Regarding the religious ethics of the early rabbinic sages and the rabbinic liturgy, see E. Uhrbach, *Hazal*, Ch. XIV. Cf. "Hatefilah Hayehudit: Hemshekh Vehidush," in Hebrew (Jerusalem: Kedem Press, 1978), especially the essay by Shalom Rosenberg, "Jewish Thought and Liturgy — Directions and Problems," pp. 85-131.

grace, that is, to be granted the fulfillment of the needs of the individual and the nation. In all of these motifs, one finds an affinity with the prayers of the prophets. This is readily apparent in the interweaving of biblical passages that constitute the liturgy. In any case, the liturgy is structured as the appearance of man before a personal God. There is no element of theophany, nor is there any element of ecstasy that lifts the praying person from his ordinary world and leads him closer to identification with a divinity.

Once again, let us emphasize that we are pointing to characteristics expressed throughout most of the literature of Oral *Torah* and of Jewish liturgy. We have no intention of concealing or denying the existence of other themes, including mystical ones. We also do not intend to conceal the existence of footholds for mystical thought, exegesis and experience, even within the public liturgy instituted by the early rabbinic sages. Indeed, a salient example of such a foothold is the distinctive "sanctification" (*kedushah*) of the *Shema* and the eighteen benedictions.[84]

In these prayers one can point to phrases that reveal the inspiration of esoteric-mystical liturgy. Such footholds will obviously be very important to people who tend to prefer an esoteric interpretation of the prayers. But since we are interested in what came to be the common and distinctive experience of the Jewish public, we focus on a liturgical corpus for which mysticism is entirely inessential. Furthermore, I must emphatically state that even the "sanctification" (*kedushah*) that furnishes a matrix for mystical experience is not mystical in and of itself. Sanctification embodies neither theophany nor ecstasy. The praying person stands among his people in his earthly reality, just as the angels stand in their heavenly reality, before a God whose presence is symbolically conveyed through the signs of the divine light. In this manner, man offers praise and thanks and accepts the authority of his sovereign God.

---

84 Compare with Ithamar Gruenwald's book, *Perakim Betoldot Yerushalayim Biymei Bayit Sheni*, in Hebrew (Jerusalem: Yad Yitzhak Ben Sevi, 1981), pp. 459-481.

This conception of prayer has, for the most part, been strictly preserved up to the present day. Distinctively mystical elements have indeed penetrated through liturgical poems located on the periphery of the standard prayer. But only the influence of Lurianic *Kabbalah* managed to lift the barrier preventing the influx of mysticism. As a result of the dissemination of Lurianic *Kabbalah,* mystical "intentions and meditations" penetrated certain versions of the liturgy. Nevertheless, as we have indicated, the broad and definitive foundations of Jewish liturgy express the experience of earthly presence before a God revealed through his word, his commandments and his governance.

The God of Israel's prayers is not in the category of an "abstract divinity." He is a living God, a father unto his sons, a king unto his slaves, who loves, ordains, leads, and judges. Max Kadushin referred to the religious experience of the prayer regulated by early rabbinic sages as "normal mysticism."[85]

This is an unsatisfactory designation because it stretches the term mysticism far beyond its range. There is no mysticism that does not strive to burst through the bounds of man's "normal" experience. For this reason, the phrase "normal mysticism" is a contradiction in terms. The prayer regulated by early rabbinic sages contains no mysticism, but it does contain the experience of presence before the concealed God within the realm of every man's ordinary earthly reality.

---

85 See Max Kadushin, *Worship and Ethics* (Chicago: Northwestern University Press, 1964).

CHAPTER 6
MYSTICISM IN MEDIEVAL JUDAISM
i. Reason, Ethics, and Asceticism

The literature of medieval Jewish thought expressed the Jewish religious consciousness in systematic and speculative form. We must dwell upon this subject at length for it is in the context of this literature that the following question emerged: what is the relation between (a) those elements that distinguished Judaism throughout its continuous history, and (b) other mystical or philosophical elements of religion. This question was analyzed in a comprehensive and systematic discussion backed throughout by methodical research.

In his scholarly writings Scholem considered two currents within the literature of medieval Jewish thought — the kabbalistic current on the one hand, and the philosophical on the other. Scholem treated "ethical literature" only parenthetically as representing a distinctive discipline or approach to the content of Jewish religion. There is an ostensible methodological reason why Scholem neglects the ethical literature. This literature is for the most part directly influenced by either philosophy or *Kabbalah*. Consequently, most ethical compositions can be treated within Scholem's aforementions dichotomous scheme of philosophy and *Kabbalah*.[86]

Yet we may also employ an approach that singles out the ethical literature as a distinctive literary genre with its own discipline. Furthermore, we may treat this literature as an expression of a particular approach to religious belief and experience.[87] The ethical literature may be influenced by *Kabbalah* or philosophy, or it may draw eclectically upon both these sources. But the essential source

86 All works reviewing the history of Jewish philosophy include essays that fall within the category of *Mussar* literature. This applies, for example, to *Hovot Halevavot, Hegyon Ha-Nefesh, Eight Chapters,* etc. . . . Despite their clear ethical character, these essays are treated as representative of scholastic philosophical approaches because of their dependence on a certain summary of philosophical ideas that derive from one philosophical school or another.

87 The beginnings of a deliberation on the definitive characteristics of this literature as a genre in its own right appears in the introduction to *A Selection of Mussar Literature,* in Hebrew, by Isaiah Tishby and Joseph Dan (Jerusalem: Neumann Publishers, 1971), and the piece by Joseph Dan appearing under the entry "Mussar, Sifrut ha . . .," in Hebrew, in the *Hebrew Encyclopedia.*

for the ethical literature may be neither philosophy nor *Kabbalah*. Rather, the source may lie in the tradition of Toraitic literature written for didactic purposes and sustaining a tight thread of succession between biblical literature and the literature of subsequent generations, by way of all the concatenations of the literature of the Oral *Torah*.

When we evaluate the literature of medieval Jewish thought from this perspective, we find very few compositions that are philosophical or mystical in the exact, disciplinary sense. Even the most famous and influential composition in medieval Jewish philosophy, namely Maimonides' *Guide for the Perplexed* it is not a philosophical essay in the disciplinary sense. Rather, it is an ethical treatise. Of course, the same applies to compositions such as Saadya Gaon's *Doctrines and Beliefs,* Bahey Ibn Pekudah's *Hovot Halevavot* or Joseph Albo's *Sefer Ha'Iqarim.* In these compositions, one can indeed isolate systematic philosophical elements. But these elements are not the focus, nor do they even always determine the structure or thematic division of the text.

The situation is slightly different in Kabbalistic literature. This literature is written in accord with a midrashic "discipline" that has its own traditional pattern. But if by "disciplinary composition" we mean a composition designed to preach a certain doctrine in a particular systematic form that reflects the internal structure of the doctrine itself, then we have only a few compositions worthy of this definition. Moreover, those works that are broadly designated as "Kabbalistic literature" are compositions designed to guide the Israelite in all aspects of his life, beliefs, and opinions. Consequently, they contain not only mystical *midrashim,* but also many of ethical literature's distinctive themes. In any case, an outlook that isolates kabbalistic, philosophical and casuistic subcurrents within the wide range of medieval ethical literature is more perspicuous than one which distinguishes three separate categories of literature: kabbalistic, philosophical and moralistic.

This argument is not only important for reasons of methodological precision. Within the context of our present discussion, it is designed to emphasize the public-didactic objective of most medieval Jewish sages. This objective governs the literature they produced. These sages' works are indeed influenced by various world views and systematic approaches, but in essence they remain faithful to the golden mean of Toraitic literature. That is, they are neither mystical nor philosophical, but rather religious-ethical.

In its purest representation, the philosophical route is oriented toward true and complete knowledge of reality. This is the highest goal for which man is destined. The religious philosopher equates this goal with the ideal of seeking God's closeness. God is the cause of everything that exists. As we perfect our knowledge of the reality that God has caused to exist, we necessarily draw nearer to knowledge of God himself. This knowledge is a love of God which, in turn, is also a closeness to God. According to this view, all actions ordained by the *Torah* were designed as means toward the single, transcendent end.

In its purest representation, the mystical route is directed toward achieving a goal that transcends cognitive knowledge. It is directed toward the unmediated experience of the eternity that encompasses all reality and permeates its depths. Therefore, this route regards the actions ordained by the *Torah* as means toward activating hidden forces that link the human being with that which is above him. These forces are activated both within the person and at the highest levels of reality. In addition to these two approaches, the philosophical and the mystical, we also find the Toraitic approach in the ethical literature.

This approach regards closeness to God as something that is achieved by fulfilling the divine ordinances with the intention of obeying a higher will. The ordinances are not considered a means to attaining a spiritual level higher than that embodied in the ordinance itself. Nor are they considered even symbols for meanings beyond human understanding. Fulfilling the ordinance is a gesture of obedience that not only expresses fear and love, but also attracts love and grace from God.

A classic expression of the appropriate means for approaching God, as understood in the medieval ethical literature, is found in the famous distinction set forth by Saadya Gaon in his book *Doctrines and Beliefs* (Saadya's work is not the first philosophical composition of medieval literature, but rather its first moralistic composition!) Saadya Gaon distinguishes between *Mitzvot Sikhliyot* ("Rational Laws") and *Mitzvot Shimi'yot* ("Revealed Laws").[88]

According to Saadya Gaon, rational laws are those which can be deduced logically from this-worldly experience by employing the criterion of pragmatic success. In other words, rational laws meet the criterion of preserving life and happiness. To exist is good. Every being yearns to perfect reality from the perspective of his own particular nature and to maintain and strengthen reality. The bad is represented in any privation or harm. The rational person, therefore, strives to sustain his existence, to perfect all aspects of his reality in accord with his nature, and to rid himself of any lack, pain or flaw that results in need or limitation. Rational morality thus affirms those actions which produce good and prevent harm in the sense defined above.

But Saadya Gaon extends this general rule to all human beings and consequently, reaches a conclusion which applies to every individual vis-a-vis the universal collectivity. So while the good is that which benefits all, an action that benefits one agent and harms another is not good. Placing individual moral judgement is a social context and thereby universalizing ethics signifies morality's rationality. The *ratio* cannot accept an action that is simultaneously both good and bad. In any case, these moral obligations can be rationally deduced by anyone, although it is fitting that a wise ruler ordain them to ensure benefits for all his subjects. Nevertheless, if someone fulfills all these obligations solely in order to achieve personal benefit, he should not yet be considered a follower

88 See Saadya Gaon's *Doctrines and Beliefs,* third essay. For an analysis of the problem, see Eliezer Schweid, *Emunah Ve-Orakh Hayim Shel Torah Lefi Rasag,* Hebrew, Studies In Jewish Thought, III (Jerusalem: n.p., 1975). Cf. *ibid., Torat Ha-Musar Ha-Datit Shel Rasag,* Hebrew, Jerusalem Studies in Jewish Thought, III, 1982.

of God. Although he may indeed fulfill God's will, such fulfillment is not his goal. Therefore his actions will not lead him to experience the proximity of God. Only those ordinances which are called *Mitzvot Shimiyot* ("revealed law") can bestow a feeling of closeness to God.

The revealed laws are not deduced from the rational analysis outlined above. Nonetheless, Saadya Gaon cautiously chooses to emphasize that divine ordinances can neither contradict reason nor bring harm or damage. Yet rational calculation alone cannot lead a man to take these obligations upon himself. They are obligatory, but only because they have been heard from the mouth of God and inscribed in his *Torah*. So a man who freely chooses to fulfill these obligations is not necessarily first weighing his own interests. Rather, he seeks to express his willingness to obey a higher will. His desire is to find favor in his creator's eyes and thereby to give thanks for the favor and grace which God has bestowed upon him. When a person fulfills the revealed law with this intention, he indeed stands before God and feels his proximity. Man's approach toward God is then reciprocated; God takes a step toward man by proclaiming commandments which enable him to express obedience and gratitude. Saadya Gaon sees this as divine grace or, if you wish, as an expression of God's personal relationship to man. Without this unique relationship, man could not possibly attain the virtue of proximity to God. The individual to whom God responds thus feels that God appeals from divine hiddenness. In this way, the person feels God's actual proximity. When fulfilling the commandment of his creator and lawgiver, he recognizes that he is loved. And the more a person fulfills such ordinances, the more he will love God and be sure of God's love for him.

Saadya Gaon therefore depicts worshipping God through fulfilling revealed law as an experience of the hidden God's tangible presence. In this description, Saadya conveys neither the philosopher's struggle for universal knowledge of truth, nor the mystic's aspiration to a sphere of eternal existence. According to Saadya Gaon the feeling of God's presence is attained in this world without changing man's normal activist inclinations and without discovering layers of reality located above that known through normal human experience. What assures that one's fulfillment of heaven's will must be answered with love? It is, in fact, the living historical memory of the exodus from Egypt and revelation at Mount Sinai, along with the other memories which evince God's leadership over his people. That is to say, the historical myth which supports the belief in uniqueness.

The term *Perishut* ("asceticism"), as understood in the medieval ethical literature, is characteristic of toraitic teaching about life patterned after divine ordinances. In both Christianity and Islam, medieval mysticism leaned toward extreme asceticism. This ascetic tendency was an implicit consequence of the following conception: in order to release the soul from its bodily shackles and to enable it to uncover the secret of its own interiority (which originates in a spiritual extra-earthly sphere), one must suppress bodily passions and subdue those bodily forces that satisfy their needs by enslaving the body.

Medieval philosophy, especially that which was influenced by Aristotle's writings, tended to modify this ascetic tendency. Its attitude to the body and to tangible reality was not quite so negative. Inasmuch as it exists, every existing thing was seen as good. But medieval philosophers also believed in a hierarchy among existing things which ranges from lesser beings affected by deficiencies and privations and governed by cycles of change, to perfect and immutable supreme beings. The material, physical creations belong to the lowest level, while the human being stands at the middle. Since he cannot alter his corporeal element, man must look after his body. But man's true purpose is located in the spiritual sphere and all his actions ought to be subordinated to realizing this purpose.

We find that the philosophers also believe that one must transcend the body's limitations and overcome its grasp upon the powers of the soul. Further, they maintain that the soul, which belongs to a higher sphere of reality, is imprisoned in the body.

107

They disagree with the mystics only as to the proper way of freeing the spirit from its bodily prison. So while the mystics tended to believe in suppressing corporeality, the philosophers maintained that corporeal existence is essential to man. They believed that one could not be released from one's body without becoming enslaved by its desires unless one satisfied them. The satiated body, which has not been accustomed to luxurious indulgence, releases the spirit and allows it to act independently. For this reason, asceticism in the philosophical sense means abstaining from luxuries and making bodily existence into a means rather than an end. A person's earthly life should be a conduit to a spiritual life that lies beyond the natural world we know through our ordinary experience.

Obviously, this distinction between the mystics' and philosophers' idea of how to live a pure spiritual life closely relates to each group's distinct conception of true spiritual life's essence. For the philosophers, spiritual life consists solely in knowing all of reality as it really is. The human mind reaches perfection and eternity when it finds the truth within itself.

The mystics, by contrast, aim to elevate the human spirit above and beyond the will. In other words, they transcend their spiritual limitations just as they transcend those of the body. This consti- tutes a radical refusal to accept their human existence. From this stems the mystic's intense and antagonistic relation to man's earthly existence in general.

But even this distinction between medieval philosophy and mysticism is not clear-cut. There was a reciprocal influence between these two currents. Indeed, the mystical ideal had such a strong influence on the philosophical ideal that ascetic tendencies filtered into the philosophers' moral doctrines. And a contrary force from philosophy can also be found in the context of mysti- cism. This force moderated the mystics' ascetic morality. Through this reciprocal influence, medieval thinkers perceived asceticism as a means to escape corporeal existence and to reach the divine presence who is beyond sinful materialism.

The ascetic stance in the Jewish ethical literature ostensibly developed through the soul's striving to reach beyond itself into a transcendent spiritual region, since it felt homeless on earth. Yet one cannot but notice that almost all the compositions which gained influence and authority among the people contain views leaning more toward the philosophical stance. Again and again one finds the directive to tread the middle path, to hold to a golden mean between the polar opposites asceticism and sensualism. One finds repeatedly the claim that halakhic norms propound a golden mean in all areas of man's physical and social life. Ascetic tendencies can be found in the ethical literature, but even in these exceptional cases one senses an awareness of the problems inherent in asceticism. For conventional wisdom clearly dictated that biblical morality rejects asceticism and looks favorably upon an earthly life that is full of satisfaction. Indeed, the medieval thinker's adherence to the view that halakhic norms represent practical applications of ideal moral principles forces the contemporary scholar to inquire whether there has not been a transformation in the interpretation of these principles themselves. He must further ask himself whether the use of terms borrowed from philosophical ethics is merely a facade concealing an entirely different approach that originates neither in mysticism nor in philosophy, but rather in *Torah*.

In order to evaluate this issue, we must return to the classic essay of Saadya Gaon. Interestingly, in the book *Doctrines and Beliefs,* the approach to asceticism (*perishut*) is ambiguous. At the start of his book's tenth section, Saadya Gaon first describes "asceticism" as an extreme monasticism which strives to crush corporeality. Immediately afterward, he vehemently rejects asceticism as a path which entirely fails to achieve its spiritual purpose.[89] He attaches a certain positive value to asceticism as a temporary means to straighten out someone who has become bound up in desire and lust, but he notes that one who perceives asceticism as a

---

89 See the tenth essay of Saadya Gaon's *Doctrines and Beliefs,* Josephuf edition (Jerusalem: 1962), Ch. IV "Shaar Ha-Perishut."

way of life becomes spiritually dull through physical suffering. Nevertheless, Saadya Gaon characterizes his entire moral teaching as "a book of asceticism."[90] In this context, asceticism is obviously given a positive interpretation for morality as a whole is taken to be "asceticism." Is this an inconsistency or an instance of dialectical thinking?

The content of the chapter in its entirety definitely indicates that the adamant rejection of monasticism is an essential matter for Saadya Gaon. This rejection derives from an affirmative and teleological perception of human life in its corporeal-terrestrial sense. Man was designed for bodily life and bodily activity. Consequently, eating, drinking, having intercourse, procreating, amassing wealth and honor, governing, exploring science, exercising wisdom and serving God all form part of what Saadya Gaon saw as the definite purpose appropriate to man. There is, of course, a hierarchical order among these activities. But it is also characteristic of Saadya Gaon that, while pointing out the reciprocal interdependence between the various functions of body and soul, he does not conceive any of these functions solely as a means for serving a higher function. Rather, he believes that all the functions together comprise the complete man. For this reason, each activity has independent value. On the other hand, the interdependence between the different functions is of a kind which requires complete reciprocity. Of course, one should not devote one's self to wisdom and service to God without satisfying prior needs and functions such as eating, drinking, the maintenance of public order, etc. Rather, the fulfilling of these needs and functions itself constitutes the realm in which man's wisdom is accumulated and revealed. Moreover, through these actions, and through them alone, can man serve his creator.

That is to say, the wisdom of which Saadya Gaon speaks is not some kind of knowledge of a reality beyond nature and natural man. Rather, it is a practical wisdom manifested in the proper

90 *Ibid.*, Ch. IV, Introduction.

organization of individual and communal life and in settling worldly affairs.

Furthermore, according to Saadya Gaon, man rules nature for his own benefit and for the benefit of the nature that God created. This is man's wisdom approximating to and imitating the creator's. For this reason, if a creature does not eat, drink, produce and raise offspring, or settle and rule the world, how is his wisdom expressed?

The same applies to the service of God. This service is nothing other than fulfilling the dictates of a higher will in affinity with the created world. The man who serves God sustains himself and the world in a manner corresponding to the creator's will, and acts with the intention of obeying his creator's commandments in all his deeds. As for the creature who does not eat and drink, procreate, educate, settle the world and govern it, in what way is he serving his God?

Through these assertions one grasps the tight connection between the rational laws and the revealed law in Saadya Gaon's moral-religious thought. Wisdom comprises the rational laws which are designed for man to use in attaining happiness. In fact, God created man so that he would adhere to this wisdom. Revealed ordinances are those which express obedience to the higher will. This constitutes the service of God. But when we follow comprehensive thought through to its logical culmination, we understand that all man's deeds are directed for his benefit. The fulfillment of revealed ordinances which elicits the willful and joyous retribution of God is no exception. All man's actions are in the service of God as long as they are performed out of a desire to obey a divine commandment. The complete man is one whose wisdom is his service, and whose service is his wisdom.

Thus the concept of "asceticism," according to a more comprehensive interpretation, signifies that it is incumbent upon man to fulfill all the functions dictated by his earthly existence so he may both live happily with the rest of humanity and fulfill his creator's wish. These are two complementary perspectives on the

111

same activity. They reflect a two-sided relation between man and his God. In fact, this understanding of the concept "asceticism" is derived neither from mysticism nor philosophy. Its foundation lies in the written *Torah* and the oral *Torah,* and in the *halakhah* which sanctifies earthly reality through a way of life governed by the divine ordinances.

In ethical works more heavily influenced by the ideals of philosophy or of mysticism, a tension which cannot be sensed in Saadya Gaon's writing is indeed generated. We shall consider two such pieces. The first, Bahey Ibn Pekudah's *Hovot Halevavot*[91] has a speculative foundation that points toward mysticism. The second, Maimonides' *Eight Chapters*, leans toward Aristotelian philosophy.

In the book *Hovot Halevavot,* one discerns a strong bias toward abstinence in that same ascetic sense which Saadya Gaon bitterly rejected. On a theoretical level, the author of *Hovot Halevavot* maintained a dichotomous distinction between the body and the soul. The body is the prison of a soul that derives from the highest spiritual sphere. Corporeal life in material earthly existence is nothing but a difficult trial, so the imprisoned soul yearns to achieve freedom and to return to its source. But in order to achieve this goal, the soul must attain self-understanding. It must also remember its original source and recognize that the earthly life is nothing but one of the lower stages on an ascending scale of reality. For this purpose, one must slowly release the soul from the firm clutch of bodily passions by gradually suppressing the desires. Ascetic abstinence is the ostensive virtue suggested by such a viewpoint.

Yet the book *Hovot Halevavot* endorses the ascetic, abstinent way of life neither for the people at large nor for the people's supreme chosen individuals. Moreover, on the basis of a sharp dialectical intuition, Bahey Ibn Pekudah even develops a contrary

---

91 For an analysis of the problem, see Eliezer Schweid, "Derekh Ha-Teshuvah Shel Hayahid Ha-metuhar — Pirkei Mehkar Be-Torat Ha-Mussar Shel Hovot Ha-Levavot," *Da'at,* Vol. I, no. 1.

motif. First of all, this-worldly life is not devoid of positive spiritual value. From the perspective of the human soul, life is a mission. The soul takes a responsibility upon itself. It thereby affirms its essential existence and gives inherent validity to this existence. The soul achieves its essence through its will and its deeds, rather than merely through the grace of the God who created it. Importantly, by accepting a missionary responsibility in relation to other existing entities, the soul realizes its freedom and acquires its own existential status. This is the crucial virtue that is attainable only in earthly life. From the perspective of earthly reality, any reality, insofar as it exists, is "good." God desires the perfection of each entity in accord with its hierarchical status. And the activity of man in his earthly life elevates reality to its highest possible level of unity and perfection. In this way, actions that bring interpersonal harmony, and activities in the realms of culture, society and polity, acquire a spiritual-religious significance. Man is perceived as a being who performs God's mission, and discovers God's grace in earthly reality. Obviously, on this base, one cannot justify an abstinence that paralyzes corporeal or creative-cultural activity. This would be a betrayal of man's mission and of the reason for his existence in the world.

We are thus dealing with a dialectical tension between two types of activity and two longings that share one root. In order to regain its original sphere of reality, the soul needs to fulfill its positive function in the world. This is its trial, but it is also its great opportunity. Through fulfilling its mission in this world, the soul can reach a higher level in the world to come. The practical solution endorsed in the book *Hovot Halevavot* focuses on the point of mutual reconciliation between these two tendencies.

The author denounces manifest, external abstinence because it entails a release from the burden of responsibility to family, to society, to the maintenance of world harmony, and even to the corporeal earthly existence of the abstaining individual himself. The author demands man's full involvement in social life and in settling worldly affairs at first for the sake of man's own development, and later on so that man may benefit ever-widening circles of his fellows.

But the overt involvement in earthly existence does not prevent covert abstinence designed to avoid enslavement of the soul to the body's desires and needs. This distinction between overt and covert abstinence may indeed seem arbitrary, but it is not so when examined from the perspective of the mature personality, i.e., one who has reached the highest degree of love and fear for God. According to the book *Hovot Halevavot,* love of God finds expression in acts of love. And what are the actions that express love of God? Doing good unto those whom God loves and whom he has therefore created and governed. So the highest level of abstinence actually consists in involvement with earthly life, though not to satisfy the desires of bodily existence, but to benefit God's creation in God's own manner. This is not withdrawal from the world, but rather withdrawal into the world. It is regarded as an assigned mission of love involving a love of God which bestows upon man the feeling of God's presence and proximity.

The believing person's path as described in *Hovot Halevavot* seems at first to overlap with the path of the mystic who subdues corporeality and withdraws to the inner and higher spheres. But when we reach the highest stages, the perspective is reversed entirely. The love of God and proximity to him are no longer conceived of in terms of the believer's withdrawal from the earthly realm either to loom in the sphere of the spiritual or to blend into it. Rather, love of God is expressed in activity that benefits earthly life. It is precisely in this manner that man lives in the presence of his creator. In this respect, Bahey Ibn Pekudah returns to the toraitic conception according to which the way to elicit God's proximity and love is to fulfill his ordinances in this world.

We also find a similar reversal of perspectives in Maimonides' ethical-religious thought. Maimonides' ethics originate from Aristotle's doctrine of the "middle path."[92] It seems, initially, that the

92 For an extensive analysis of this issue, see Eliezer Schweid, *Iyunim Be-Shemonah Perakim La-Rambam* (Jerusalem: Jewish Agency Publications, 1965), Ch. IV.

Maimonidean *telos* is identical with the Aristotelian philosophers' ideal of perfection, perfect knowledge of all that exists inasmuch as it can be known to man. All of man's actions should be means to this end, whether by way of preparing environmental conditions, or through the processes of learning themselves. In order to devote one's self to a life of rational activity, and in order to attain constancy in the state of actual knowledge, it is necessary to break free, as far as possible, from the grip of bodily passions and needs. The exclusive devotion to a single aim bestows upon Maimonides' philosophical ethics the character of an ascetic orientation which leans at certain points toward a measure of fanaticism (such is the case with respect to Maimonides' attitude to sexual satisfaction!).

However, even in the writings of Maimonides one finds the same dialectical tension that dispatches the perfectly wise man to earthly life to perform beneficial actions in this world and thereby to become a servant and lover of God. This is what actually distinguishes between the image of the wise man as an ideal of philosophical perfection and the image of the prophet as an ideal of religious perfection. In the final analysis, it is not the wise man in the Aristotelian sense but rather the prophet who serves as the ideal image to which Maimonides aspires in both his *Eight Chapters* and his *Guide for the Perplexed*.[93] The prophet is a messenger and a leader. Upon reaching his highest level, he turns to the community of humans in order to lead them in their earthly reality. His role is to instill mercy, justice and righteousness on earth. The prophet thus imitates his God and expresses his awareness and recognition that God is the creator and governor of the world. And proximity and love of God are perceived by the prophet in the fulfillment of God's ordinances and *Torah*.

Finally, we should consider one last medieval composition that attained the status of a classic, Judah Halevi's *Book of the Kuzari*. This book requires attention since it comprises its time's clearest attempt to express both the historical myth of Judaism and the quest for closeness to God through *Torah* and divine ordinances.

93 *Ibid.*, Ch. VII.

Whoever examines it in depth will find that it internalizes the ideals of mystical and philosophical religiosity.

Judah Halevi describes the prophet as a man who has a system of internal senses enabling him to experience a spiritual presence in just the same manner that a normal man experiences a tangible one. He also upholds prophecy as the direct experience of a metaphysical presence between man and his God. Judah Halevi thus bestows upon prophecy a distinctly mythical-mystical dimension.[94]

By contrast, when he adopts the golden mean as his major principle of ideal human government, and when he encourages the study of natural wisdom as part of the human perfection preceding spiritual-religious perfection, he is also bestowing a scientific-philosophical dimension upon the traditional teaching of *Torah*.

However, Judah Halevi's synthesis falls entirely within the conceptual realm of the toraitic-prophetic tradition, which is neither mystical nor philosophical. He bitterly rejects the path of mystical asceticism as well as the philosophers' path of isolation for the sake of contemplation. As far as he is concerned, closeness to God is achieved in the totality of the Israelite's way of life in this world, and in a specifically social context. Man can be a servant of God in all his actions — as long as all his actions are performed in accordance with the *Torah*. Furthermore, even though Judah Halevi described the experience of God's nearness as a presence expressing a mystical dimension, nevertheless he emphasizes alertness and willful-readiness on the part of the man who stands prepared at all times to fulfill his creator's wishes.[95] Indeed, this very preparedness places man in the state where a metaphysical experience of divine presence will occur.

94 The discussion of this issue appears in the fourth chapter of R. Judah Ha-Levi's *Book of the Kuzari*.
95 *Ibid.*, Ch. III.

ii. Philosophy and Kabbalah

In light of the foregoing discussion, it behooves us to re-examine Scholem's view of medieval and modern Jewish philosophy's contribution to Judaism's development. Scholem prefers the mystical route over the philosophical one. He sees mysticism as the only authentic religious solution. Indeed, he treats philosophy as an inauthentic substitute for religion. His preference for mysticism is based on arguments that resemble the polemics directed against the "philosophers" by earlier defenders of the Jewish faith, both Kabbalists and non-Kabbalists. These arguments formed part of the controversy surrounding Maimonides' *Guide for the Perplexed.* The controversy first broke out in the beginning of the thirteenth century and flared up time and again throughout the subsequent centuries. Of course, these polemics were not groundless insofar as they referred to the attitude of many philosophers to life governed by *Torah* and divine ordinances. Even if philosophy was not, as polemicists claimed, the cause of licentiousness, it did in any case provide sufficiently convenient and sharply defined excuses for those who, for particular social-cultural reasons, leaned toward casting off the yoke of moral and religious responsibility.[96]

We must not, however, overlook the fact that similar arguments were directed against the Kabbalists and their tradition. We have already noted above that mysticism either caused or provided the pretext for several crises. Moreover, these crises were far more severe than those for which the philosophers were blamed. But one can also argue that mysticism actually served a sustaining function, for these severe crises were caused by movements which expressed an extraordinary intensity of religious sentiment. Philosophy, by its essential nature, neither expressed nor generated such sentiment.

As long as mysticism was strictly confined to the context of a concealed teaching transmitted quietly and exclusively to worthy

---

96 A detailed description of this reality appears in Fritz Baer's *History of the Jews in Christian Spain,* Ch. III, paragraph IV.

individuals, it succeeded more than philosophy in fortifying a religious leadership that was faithful to the ways of *Torah*.

Mysticism was more successful than philosophy in persuading God-fearing Jews that its bold innovations were the deep intention of the *Torah* revealed at Sinai. Mysticism was also more successful than philosophy in renewing the experiential religious significance of studying the *Torah* and fulfilling its commandments. Finally, mysticism was more successful than philosophy in sustaining the belief of God-fearing Jews in the veracity of the historical myth that comprised the exodus from Egypt, the revelation of *Torah,* and the hopes for redemption at the end of the exile. Obviously, a religious movement based on a myth will be more successful in fulfilling these tasks than a mode of thinking that stands in essential confrontation with the mythological mode of thought. Jewish philosophy did, in fact, go to great lengths to preserve and sustain the historical myth without contradicting its own scientific-rationalistic foundations. But it must be admitted that the philosophers only succeeded in this endeavor with great difficulty. In principle, because of the historical foundation of the prophetic toraitic myth, this task was not impossible. However, the mytho-logical motif that emerges from the experiential-supernatural dimension posed a major difficulty. How can one reconcile a miraculous occurrence that violates the laws of nature with a philosophical view which equates the laws of nature with the laws of the *ratio?* It is not surprising that the philosophers' various solutions to this dilemma generated mistrust. By contrast, for the *Kabbalah,* which is anchored in supernatural myth, there is noth-ing more natural than the miracle. Indeed, for *Kabbalah,* the serious difficulty is rooted in the fact that miracles which should occur do not occur for the people of Israel in their diasporic present. This needs to be explained by the *Kabbalah.*

Setting this aside, it is clear why *Kabbalah* was more successful than philosophy in facilitating direct communication between the religious leadership and the people. Mystical religion was not identical with the spiritual temperament of the people, yet there was an affinity between the two. The philosophical stance, on the other hand, generated an aristocracy that was not only isolated but also alienated from the masses. Finally, one clearly would not anticipate that philosophy should disseminate and penetrate into the popular religion, as mysticism did following the expulsion from Spain.

Nevertheless, Scholem's decisive verdict against philosophy evidently represents a simplistic approach to this entire set of issues. Let us begin with his central argument against philosophy, his claim that even in its Jewish theological formulation, philosophy was nothing but a pseudo-religious substitute. Scholem's arguments pertaining to this issue usually revolved around Maimonides' theology. We shall likewise devote our attention to an analysis of Maimonides' central, influential case. Did Maimonides truly comprehend the ideas of creation, revelation, providence and redemption — as well as the rationale of the divine ordinances — in a fashion that emptied these concepts of their experiential-religious content?[97]

Although Scholem does not say so explicitly, his discussion of this issue begins with the assumption that, at least methodologically, all philosophy can be defined according to the two classical models that influenced the various schools of medieval philosophy. These two models come from Plato and Aristotle. Further, Scholem seems to accept a view that was indeed quite prevalent during the middle ages. This view presupposes that Aristotle's philosophy was the philosophy with a capital "P."

The Platonic and Aristotelian models are the most mature product of pagan intellectualism. For this reason, the encounter between *Torah* and philosophy can reasonably be regarded as a confrontation between a religious worldview in the monotheistic sense and a pagan worldview. Furthermore, the pagan worldview may be regarded simply as "non-religious" if we evaluate it according to the toraitic-religious criterion.

97 For an analysis of this issue, see Julius Guttman, "The Religious Motifs in Maimonides' Philosophy," *Religion and Knowledge,* Hebrew (Jerusalem: Magnes, 1955).

Even if we accept the assumption behind this simplistically conceived confrontation, questions still arise. First, does the philosophy that developed in a pagan context nevertheless carry in its midst certain experiential elements which can be defined as "religious"? Moreover, do these elements not stand in a complex relationship with experiential-religious elements of the *Torah*? Is it not incorrect to perceive this relationship in terms of an absolute rejection? But as far as we are concerned, the more important problem is which definition correctly distinguishes the characteristics and components of the philosophies that developed within the institutional frameworks of the Jewish, Christian and Islamic religions during the middle ages. Do these philosophies truly represent a simple (albeit less "clear" and "consistent") continuation of the classical Greek models? Or is it perhaps worth discussing a certain variety of medieval philosophies which can be seen as philosophical approaches with unique characteristics?

In other words, is it not worth asserting with regard to philosophy what Scholem claims for mysticism? Scholem, as we recall, maintains that there is no single, continuous mysticism, but rather each institutional religion has its own mysticism. If this is the case, is it not also true that there is no single, continuous philosophy? Is it not true that each distinctive culture and religion, when the appropriate time arrives, acquires its own philosophy? The concept of "philosophy" is indeed unitary insofar as it refers to the demand for thought on a critical-conceptual plain. Philosophical thought also provides a full account of its considerations, and strives to prove the validity of its arguments and conclusions. But philosophy may also be seen as a systematic, critical, elaborated summary of certain contents derived from particular experiences in a natural and historical-cultural environment. In this case, there can be no unitary philosophy, and no philosophy can represent "*the* philosophy." Rather, each culture has its own philosophy and each religion has its own religious philosophy — provided, of course, that through its history the culture or religion is held accountable on a conceptual-critical level.[98]

The differences between various philosophies can thus be just as great as the differences between various mysticisms. Within this wide spectrum, there may develop non-religious philosophies and pseudo-religious philosophies. We may even find philosophies that elevate the most authentic religious thought and experience to the level of pure conceptual observation. Modern philosophy of the nineteenth and twentieth centuries, contains several distinct examples of non-religious philosophy. It also contains distinct instances of pseudo-religious philosophy, which is nothing but a secular substitute for religion. But there certainly are philosophical systems that succeeded in internalizing the religious dimension within which they developed. Moreover, these philosophical systems express an experience of divine presence no less real and intense than the one found in mysticism, even though we are obviously dealing with essentially different types of religious experience.

Maimonides' religious philosophy is a distinct example of this type of religious philosophy. In Maimonides' thought, philosophy is the authentic route toward the experience of God's presence. Furthermore, philosophy constitutes an integral part of a comprehensive religious way of life which corresponds to a comprehensive systematic worldview. In the present context, we cannot provide a detailed discussion of the religious experience articulated in *Guide for the Perplexed* and in other Maimonidean treatises. However, we can point to two different perspectives that he brings to bear upon this issue.[99]

The two perspectives are alluded to in Maimonides' 'doctrine of attributes.' This doctrine brings the discussion of the first part of

---

98 In connection with our discussion, there is special significance to the fact that a philosopher who belongs to the reform "rationalist" trend of nineteenth-century Jewish thought developed such an approach to religious philosophy. We refer to Samuel Hirsch. Cf. Eliezer Schweid, *Toledot Hehagut Hayehudit Ba-Et Ha-Hadashah,* Ch. VII.

99 For a detailed analysis of this issue, see Eliezer Schweid, "Hasagat Elohim Ba-Mahshavah" in *Feeling and Speculation* (Ramat-Gan: Massadah, 1970).

Guide for the Perplexed to its climax and leads the reader toward the experience of divine presence in two interrelated and mutually complementary ways.

On the one hand, there is an experience of divine presence achieved by way of the illumination of truth that transcends metaphysics. When thought both exhausts its capacity to comprehend and perceives its own limits, it confronts that which is beyond its comprehension. This perception also constitutes a real experience which parallels that described by mystical writers influenced by neo-platonism.

On the other hand, there is the experience of divine presence achieved through knowing God's attributes as a leading, creating, legislating and supervising personality. This presence is expressed in behavior imitating those divine attributes through which God reveals himself in his world (in acts of compassion, justice, and righteousness in the society of humans).[100]

In this way, as we recall, Maimonides draws nearer to the experience of divine presence based on a way of life governed by *Torah* and divine ordinances. The fulfillment of divine ordinances out of a yearning to imitate God in his government of the world constitutes closeness to God and love of God.

Scholem argues that Maimonides' teaching of the rationale behind the divine ordinances portrays the ordinances of the *Torah* as if they were nothing other than didactic exercises guiding man toward concentration on speculative activity. It is true that the divine ordinances are understood by Maimonides as a preparation for the speculative life. This holds true especially with regard to ordinances that are ritualistic in character and mythological in origin, such as the sacrificial ordinances. These ordinances are given a historical rationale, rather than a mythological one. In Maimonides' view, they were designed to distance the Israelites from the idolatry that prevailed in their environment. It is true that the

---

100 This aspect of Maimonides' thought was emphasized especially by Hermann Cohen. We must admit that Hermann Cohen's interpretation is one-sided. But there is no doubt that he redresses a common oversight on the part of modern scholars concerning a most central element of Maimonides' religious system.

Kabbalah provides these commandments with an independent, positive rationale, but in his particular relation to ritualistic ordinances, did Maimonides stand very far from the teaching of the later prophets? And were Maimonides' statements concerning these particular ordinances intended to refer to all of the ordinances?

Maimonides found independent, positive justifications for the political and social-ethical ordinances (which are designed to produce compassion, justice, and worldly righteousness) as well as for the prayers, festivals and appointed times. Moreover, his justifications express a real sense of closeness to God for each person according to his own level. Indeed, it must be stressed in this connection that Maimonides does not regard the standard prayers required of each Jew as "exercise" for metaphysical speculation. Prayer does not fulfill this role for sages, and certainly not for other Jews. As far as Maimonides is concerned, prayer is a direct emotional expression of the love and fear of God. His clearest and most intensive discussion of this issue, which appears at the beginning of the second chapter of *Hilkhot Yesodei HaTorah,* applies to every God-fearing person of Israel, rather than to the sages alone.[101] Within the standard prayer, Maimonides found that same dialectical emotional tension between love and fear which the greatest of sages experience in their speculation.

The same type of argument applies to Scholem's claim that Maimonides neutralized the utopian dimension in the prophetic idea of messianism, thereby transforming it into a kind of allegory. It is true that Maimonides sharply distinguishes between "the world to come" (a supreme metaphysical ideal for human beings) and "the days of the messiah" (a historical ideal that is nothing other than a means for attaining the supreme metaphysical ideal). It is true that, on the basis of this distinction, Maimonides took from "the days of the messiah" the miraculous and apocalyptic dimensions expressed in some early rabbinic writings that were appropriated by the *Kabbalah.*

---

101 Maimonides, *Sefer Ha-Mada La-Rambam,* "Hilkhot Yesodei Ha-Torah," Ch. II.

According to Maimonides, the "days of the Messiah" designate historical events that do not transcend the limits of natural possibility. But even on this issue, Maimonides is consistently loyal to the religious-ethical thought of the late prophets and to parts of the early rabbinic corpus. Moreover, Maimonides does not neglect the utopian-futuristic dimension of the messianic idea. Nor does he neglect the supra-terrestrial dimension of the religious ideal of life. Indeed the contrary is the case. Not only do Maimonides' writings (particularly his legal essays) provide halakhic depictions of the messianic age, his depictions are more worthy of the title "halakhic" than any other messianic descriptions found in the religious thought of medieval sages. His descriptions do not contain a miraculous dimension in the sense of a change in the order of nature. This is in keeping with the principles of halakhic utopia, since *halakhah* does not predicate its regulative principles upon miracles, but rather upon the nature of human beings and the circumstances of their actual-earthly existence. But nevertheless, Maimonides' portrait of the political and social-ethical perfection of the days of the messiah represents a distinct utopianism that is separated from the miraculous by a boundary as fine as a thread of hair.

One can provide an instructive comparison that highlights several key points by juxtaposing Maimonides' description of the days of the messiah with his writings on the prophecy of Moses, the ideal *halakhic* leader.[102] As interpreted by Maimonides, prophecy represents the natural perfection of man. In its own right, prophecy contains no supernatural element, except for the fact that the prophet exhausts his natural capacity in an effort to attain a perfection that transcends human capacity. This is the supernatural dimension or, if you wish, the miraculous dimension that is uniquely manifested in the personality of Moses.

Moses was the greatest of the prophets. He exhausted the human capacity to the point of perfection. In other words, Moses is the ideal model of the perfect man. He was not more than a man,

102 Maimonides, *Eight Chapters,* Ch. VII.

but within the framework of natural possibilities in our material world, it is certainly well known that the perfection of natural potential transcends the scope of the natural. This is why there has never arisen another prophet like Moses. This one-time manifestation of perfection is a unique miracle. Furthermore, this miracle was brought about specifically in order to bring into the world an ideal political and social-ethical law-code. The code portrays the ideal of perfection. Like Moses himself, the Written *Torah* that he handed down is a model. It defines a routine of life which exhausts the range of perfection. Man can attain ideal perfection in theory, but not in practice. Thus, the Oral *Torah* is required as a means to bridge the gap between this ideal and the possibilities dictated by the given natural and historical conditions.

Here we find our proper context for interpreting Maimonides' writings on "the days of the messiah." The messiah-king is not an ideal legislator like Moses, but he is the ideal governor who establishes a perfect mode of life in accord with *Torah*. Through the messiah, every Jew has the privilege of attaining the highest degree of spiritual-religious perfection that he is capable of achieving. In theory, this perfection represents the realization of a potentiality that inheres in human nature. Consequently, the achievement of this perfection should contain no miraculous dimension. Nevertheless, the achievement of this kind of perfection transcends the limits of natural perfection. Thus, there exists no greater miracle than such an achievement. Maimonides' messianic ideal is, therefore, a distinct utopia. He exhausts the limits of historical possibility in his struggle to reach a supra-terrestrial and supra-historical ideal.

Did Maimonides believe that the days of the messiah would actually take place at the "end of days" according to the image sketched in his writings? There is indeed room for some controversy here. But if we take upon ourselves to draw conclusions from what we find in his explicit writings, our question must definitely be answered affirmatively. The belief in the coming of the messiah is posited as a foundation in all Maimonides' toraitic-halakhic essays. His belief is founded on a prior belief that supreme providence is revealed in the history of the Jewish people. The clear manifestations of this providence are the exodus from Egypt, Sinaitic revelation, and the *Torah*. The *Torah* manifests divine providence insofar as it represents an ideal way of life which was revealed at Sinai. All those who live and behave in accord with the *Torah*'s way of life are thus placed under a divine governance that has a clear historical purpose. To this material, we may add Maimonides' writings on the continuous struggle between the idolatrous peoples and the people of Israel who remain faithful to the *Torah*. This struggle consists of various stages. According to Maimonides, the days of the Messiah signify both the final victory in this struggle and the point of greatest convergence between historical reality and the halakhic ideal of *Torah*.[103] In all these respects, Maimonides remains quite consistently faithful to the messianic ideal of the prophets and to the historical myth emptied of its apocalyptical and mystical motifs.

The distinction Scholem suggests between the symbolic interpretation of *Kabbalah* and the allegorical interpretation of the Maimonidean school raises a complex set of issues that cannot be dealt with in detail here. But at the very least, it is worth noting that such a schematic and clear-cut distinction is simplistic. The *Kabbalah* did indeed produce a rich and distinctive "dictionary" of symbols, but in a large segment of the interpretations found in the books of *Kabbalah,* including the book of *Zohar,* this symbolic dictionary was put to use in a distinctly allegorical way. Furthermore, the kabbalists' use of allegory is often mechanistic. That is to say, the allegorical usage constantly repeats a standard set of identifications.

Scholem may be correct to claim that the mystic posits the existence of an essential connection between the literal body of the symbol and the reality to which it alludes or which it activates in

---

103 This follows from the contrast of Maimonides' writings on the issue of the messiah between his message to the Jews of Yemen, and his code, *Mishneh Torah,* "Hilkhot Melakhim," Ch. XI.

the higher spheres. However one cannot ignore that there is a distinctly allegorical relation between the plain meaning of the interpreted texts and the significance assigned to them according to the symbolic "dictionary" of the *Kabbalah*. Furthermore, the work of "translation" from one realm of understanding to another is mostly mechanical and often even arbitrary. For this reason, the spiritual process expressed in the creation and study of these interpretations is not essentially different from that expressed in the creation and study of philosophical allegory. Both the interpreter and the student require a conceptual network that mediates between the body of the symbol and the higher spiritual significance attached to it. This mediating network is found neither in the uninterpreted text nor in its explication. Rather, it is found in the scholastic tradition that shapes the interpretative mode of thought.

On the other hand, one must not follow Scholem in ignoring the symbolic dimensions found in the allegorical interpretation of Maimonides and his students. According to Maimonides' theory, prophecy requires a particularly strong and sensitive imaginative capacity. The prophet's unique and wonderful imaginative capacity enables him to provide visual illustrations of metaphysical perceptions. Only the prophets are capable of adequately illustrating metaphysical perceptions. Even though each prophet may have his own individual style, there is in any case a singular and unique connection between the prophetic metaphor and its metaphysical content.

This idea is particularly emphasized in the sharp distinction that Maimonides draws between prophetic metaphors and the metaphors of the liturgical poets *(paytanim)*. The prophetic metaphor is adequate, and therefore legitimate in the context of popular toraitic instruction. The metaphors of the liturgical poets are not adequate, and should therefore be avoided.[104] This distinction is not merely the consequence of a preference for maximal restraint in the popular use of metaphors, especially in sacred liturgical poetry.

104 See Maimonides, *Guide for the Perplexed,* Part I, ch. 59.

Maimonides explicitly notes that the prophetic metaphor has a special quality that renders it fit to illustrate metaphysical truths appropriately. Consequently, anyone who appeals to these metaphors, even if he is not a philosopher, finds himself oriented and guided toward perception of the truth. Therefore, the allegorical interpretations of prophetic visions also contain a symbolic dimension that does not differ greatly in character from kabbalistic symbolism. Thus, there is a symbolic dimension in Kabbalistic interpretation and an allegorical dimension in philosophical interpretation. And if one wishes to posit a deep essential-methodological distinction between these two ways of thinking, as did Scholem, one must significantly refine the tools for distinguishing between the symbolic and allegorical dimensions in both kabbalistic and philosophical interpretation.

We cannot satisfactorily complete our examination of the relative positions of philosophy and *Kabbalah* within Judaism's history without examining both philosophy's independent value as a cultural creation and the role it filled within the wider context of Jewish culture in general. Scholars who study the history of Israel's people and their culture agree that philosophy was not an original creation produced in the cultural circles of the Jewish people. Philosophy should not be portrayed as a direct development of either biblical or early rabbinic thought.

It is well known and quite obvious that Jewish philosophy would not have developed if the people of Israel had not crossed the paths of Greece and Rome and if the sages of Israel had not come into close contact with Islamic and Christian counterparts who, in their own way, accepted Greek philosophy's influence. Or, at least, there would be no Jewish philosophy in that methodological sense implied by the Greek term *philosophia*. To begin with, philosophy was created in the cultural sphere of the Jewish people as a response to an external influence that expressed an essential feature of other cultures. It is obvious that a response to such influences creates intense tensions. Philosophy forms part of a response to the challenge posed by elements that are "different," "contrary," and "alien." But for precisely this reason, Jewish philosophy played a vital role in the continuing development of Jewish culture. From the moment philosophy was needed, albeit as a response to an external challenge, it could not be foresaken. From that point on, the need for philosophy was internalized.[105]

Philosophy is, first and foremost, a cultural creation of independent value. It exhaustively develops a certain layer of creativity that expresses the relation between man's inner world and his environment. There is no high culture that does not develop this stratum in its own way. There are some cultures in which the development of this layer is vitally necessary for preserving their creative integrity in other strata as well. Cultures based upon scientific thinking, and the accumulation of scientific knowledge depend upon philosophy. At a particular stage in their development, such cultures become unable to relinquish philosophy. The people of Israel entered the sphere of influence of such a culture, first during the days of the second Temple, and later on, during the middle ages.

From the medieval period up to the present day, the Jewish people has been mostly located within the realm of a western culture which is based on scientific thinking and the accumulation of scientific knowledge. The people sought to participate in the culture of its environment, to exist in this environment and to make its contribution, while also preserving its individuality and uniqueness. The Jewish people therefore needed sciences, scientific thought, and philosophy. Once again, we are pointing to a challenge that derived from an external source. But a positive response to an external challenge is among the conditions for the development of an independent culture. We are therefore dealing in this case with a need that became internalized. We can state categorically that from the tenth century, it became apparent to Jewish thinkers that philosophy was vitally necessary for the continuity of Jewish culture's integral development — insofar as Judaism did

105 Compare with the writings of Julius Guttmann on this issue in the introduction to his book, *The History of Jewish Philosophy*.

not relinquish its aspiration to remain the comprehensive culture of a people.

Philosophy thus developed as a response to an overall cultural need rather than merely as a struggle against a crisis from the realms of "faith" and "religious life" in their limited sense. In fact, there was a close connection between the crisis in religious life and the overarching cultural need. We refer to the cultural need evoked through interaction with the overall environment that determined the basic conditions of economic, social, and political existence in all of their scientific and cultural implications. Philosophy was called upon as a means to address this need. In this way, philosophy became internalized as a vital dimension of religious life. One can neither understand the development of philosophy nor appreciate its contribution unless one locates philosophy within a larger context, the people of Israel and the other peoples in its environment.

In this context, it is worth redetermining a fact that has been proven time and again in Jewish history. We have already noted how the development of mysticism was also generated by the encounter with an influential cultural environment. But it should be pointed out that mysticism never succeeded in coping with the full range of this problematic intercultural encounter. Mysticism solved the problem only on the plane of religion, in the limited theological and ritualistic sense. Mysticism succeeded in these areas by enabling the Jew who remained faithful to his religion and its sources to draw nearer to the religious language of his immediate surroundings. This facilitated a confrontation based on a minimum of mutual understanding.

But mysticism was unable to assist the Jew who sought to remain faithful to his religion while also comprehending or locating his place within European civilization. Mysticism did indeed attempt to provide its adherents with both an orientation and an ability to influence the circumstances in which they found themselves during the middle ages and on the eve of the new period. But to this purpose, mysticism was able to employ only fantastical means that did not describe immanent reality. Furthermore, mysticism did not relate to the conceptual framework through which the surrounding civilization defined reality, its conditions and its laws. For this reason, mysticism actually brought about an ever-deepening isolation of the people of Israel from its environment. Ultimately, mysticism also led to the fundamentally catastrophic effort to confront actual reality with entirely irrelevant means.

To this day, one finds people who assume that the Kabbalist can control historical reality by activating a symbolic apparatus which "influences" the lower spheres through stimulating higher spiritual forces. This is an exciting prospect which enriches the imagination and awakens the romantic sentiment even in our day. One may very strongly believe in a real link between spiritual activation and higher factors that influence earthly reality. Furthermore, this belief may indeed help the believer to overcome the crisis inherent in his feeling that God, as a governor of history, has concealed his visage. But it represents nothing but a solution by means of an internalization that ignores actual historical reality. Therefore, in all important respects, this solution is a crippling illusion.

From the very outset, any attempt to subject this belief to the test of real history — and every mystical movement tended to make such an attempt — necessarily leads to the destruction of an entire world of hope and results in complete despair. That is to say, a culture will neither develop nor preserve its individuality unless it can both relate objectively to its environment and carry on a dialogue with neighboring civilizations. Further, this dialogue must employ the conceptual language in which those civilizations define the conditions and rules of their economic, social, political, and scientific activity. In fact, it was only through philosophy that such an interaction with the surrounding environment was facilitated during the middle ages and the early modern period. This was philosophy's clear advantage over mysticism.

In short, both mysticism and philosophy developed in Judaism as a response to external influence and out of a struggle with difficulties generated by the cultures and religions which surrounded the people of Israel. While mysticism had an advantage over philosophy in confronting this religious crisis in its immediate theological and experiential sense, philosophy had an advantage over mysticism in the confrontation with the overall civilization to which the people of Israel had to adapt itself in order to exist. Both mysticism and philosophy were internalized and, over the course of time, became vital components of the religious and cultural creation that we call "Judaism." Within Judaism both philosophy and mysticism generated strong tensions and represented dangerous realms.

A comprehensive view of the Jewish religion cannot overlook either mysticism or philosophy, for these are not simply two delimited and differentiated movements within the history of the Jewish religion. Rather, these movements influenced one another and affected other forms and modes in which Jews have understood and experienced their religion since the middle ages. But the scholar who ponders the secret of the Jewish religion's continuity and singularity will not find this secret in mysticism or in philosophy. Rather, he will find it in the historical myth of the Bible and the early rabbinic sages, and in the religious experience that comes to expression in the way of life based on that historical myth, namely, the life of *Torah* and divine ordinances. This is the thread of continuity that runs from the Bible and prophecy to the enterprise of early rabbinic sages, from the works of early rabbinic sages to the creations of the medieval sages, from the creations of these sages to the products of the Jewish religion's sages and thinkers in the modern age.

CHAPTER 7

MYSTICISM IN MODERN JUDAISM

i. The Role of Sabbatianism

We now approach our final issue, Scholem's relation to *Wissenschaft des Judentums* and to religious Jewish thought which sought to confront the problems of the Jewish religion in the aftermath of the crisis of emancipation. Three sets of issues will be included in this part of our discussion:

1. The role of Sabbatianism within the history of the Jewish religion. The function of this movement as a transitional phenomenon within the continuous flow of Jewish religious life from the middle ages to the modern age. Or, Sabbatianism as an early manifestation of the crisis of emancipation and as a nurturing source for thinkers who began to confront this crisis.
2. The role that Scholem assigns to mysticism in overcoming the crisis that emerged with the emancipation.
3. The value of modern religious Jewish thought of the eighteenth, nineteenth, and twentieth centuries. That is, the significance of thinking generated through diverse efforts to solve the contemporary problems of the Jewish religion.

Scholem described the Sabbatian movement as the climax of a messianic-apocalyptic wave that derived its power from the myth of Lurianic *Kabbalah*. After this tradition was disseminated in the public domain, it became a formative element of popular Jewish religion throughout the dispersions of the Jewish people. To be sure, the ascent toward the climax of a mass, popular messianic movement entailed a dialectical change in the tradition of Lurianic *Kabbalah*. Formerly, it had been seen as a messianism that did not strive for direct activity on a historical plane. Lurianic messianism had represented an effort to bring the days of the messiah nearer by "repair" of the world through the fulfillment of divine injunctions in accord with the appropriate intentions. This messianism was transformed into a historically vigorous force that actively strove to deliver the people from exile.[106] In this activist tendency and in the urgent inclination to burst through the walls of the ghetto immediately, one finds the features that link Sabbatianism with the modern period of Jewish history. Furthermore, Sabbatianism expressed the internal pressure created by existence within the framework of the halakhic way of life which distinguished the Jew from his surroundings. It also expressed the characteristically modern effort to break out of this confinement and to reach the open re alm of the social and cultural life that had begun to reveal itself in the surrounding European environment. This desire was indeed unveiled when Sabbatianism reached its breaking point. The paradox of the converted messiah symbolically embodied the longing to 'redeem' the Jewish people from the confinement of exile, even through the destruction of its foundations.[107]

Scholem's outlook regards Sabbatianism as the first embodiment generated by the tragic dialectic of the crisis of modernity. Sabbatianism is thus established as a central event. But according to Scholem, Sabbatianism does not derive its centrality solely from its definitive demarcation of the boundary between periods. Rather, Sabbatianism is central because it acted as a catalyst for historical forces that continued to be active among the Jewish people beyond the demarcated boundary. Sabbatianism destroyed the reign of Judaism's religious tradition. For this purpose, Sabbatianism made use of massive forces that were derived from the tradition itself. Consequently, this shattering destruction actually represents a continuation and catalysis of internal forces that continued to shape Judaism in the modern era. This is the deep dialectical tension inherent in the paradox of a "*mitzvah* ('ordained virtue') achieved through sin," or of redemption accomplished through destruction.

106 See *Sabbatai Sevi*, Ch. I.
107 Scholem himself sharply emphasized this motif in his famous essay "Redemption Through Sin." He also repeats these claims in his book on Sabbatai Sevi, Volume II, Ch. VII.

In Scholem's opinion, this same paradoxical dialectic is embodied in the spiritual movements that arose after Sabbatianism in order to confront the crisis of diasporic life. Furthermore, these movements were embossed with the stamp of Sabbatianism not merely insofar as they had to overcome it. These movements even derived their momentum from Sabbatianism and internalized elements of its dialectical message of the "virtue achieved through sin." Such movements include:

1. Hassidism, which, in Scholem's view, arose from a strong internal connection with the Sabbatian crisis.[108]
2. The Jewish enlightenment (*haskalah*), which responded positively to the expansion of external horizons and thereby continued the Sabbatian outward-oriented eruption (in Scholem's opinion, the Frankists and the early figures of the Jewish enlightenment were linked together not only on a conceptual and ideational level, but also on the level of personal connections between specific individuals).[109]
3. Zionism, a movement generated out of the Jewish enlightenment, but which must also be seen as a dialectical continuation of Jewish messianism which sought to redeem Judaism and to preserve it through revolutionary change — though it was itself wrought with internal contradictions.[110]

We are thus dealing with three movements that adopted three different orientations in order to sustain the history of the Jewish people in the modern era: But these three share a single root, the Kabbalistic-messianic myth that underwent a process of catalysis resulting from the Sabbatian avalanche that had breached the core of the myth. Scholem argues that the crisis of entering the secular reality of modernity is the most severe crisis ever encountered by Judaism. This argument is clarified through the aforementioned depiction of Sabbatianism as a symbolic event. However, at the same time, Scholem also argues that this crisis will be overcome

---

108 See *Major Trends*, ninth lecture; cf. "The Neutralization of the Messianic Element in Early Hassidism" in *The Messianic Idea*.
109 See footnote 33.
110 See footnote 28.

only through the renewal of a mystical movement which will rise up from the depths in which the crisis occurred. This argument itself fits the internal model of the Lurianic *Kabbalah* out of which Sabbatianism erupted.

This is a dialectical outlook. It returns to Lurianic *Kabbalah*. From this vantage point, one views the events that transpired after the Lurianic tradition had broken down in face of a historical reality that it could no longer describe in its own terms. Such an outlook will clearly portray the breakdown of Lurianic *Kabbalah* and the detachment from this tradition as events marking the start of a new progression. That which carved out the abyss is destined to refill it.

At this point, Scholem's historical-philosophical outlook reflects Isaac Luria's *Kabbalah*. Lurianic *Kabbalah* interprets the great debacles that occurred in Jewish history (the sin of the golden calf, the destruction of the first Temple, etc.) as turning points that brought about total redemption. The deeper the fall, the deeper the point from which redemption can begin to "generate." But this dialectical view also draws direct support from Scholem's idea of mysticism's role within the Jewish religion. The proximity between Lurianic *Kabbalah* and Scholem's view is also the result of parallel structures of thought. But whatever the case, we are clearly dealing here with a presupposition that is not susceptible to scholarly-historical verification. Scholem devoted great efforts to provide a scientific basis for his historical intuition. His accomplishments in this area are less impressive than any of his other achievements.

Scholem did succeed in demonstrating that several sages from the original circle that generated Hassidism were influenced by or personally connected with Sabbatianism. He also proved that the founders of Hassidism were gravely concerned with curing the Sabbatian affliction. It does not follow, however, that Hassidism, insofar as it was a movement of spiritual renewal, derived some of its positive content from Sabbatianism. At the very most, this suggests that Sabbatianism was one of the phenomena that

136

characterized the dangerous reality which the founders of Hassidism sought to confront. In this instance, we at least have a factual basis for the claim that there was some historical connection between the two movements. As for the Jewish enlightenment, there is even less factual evidence suggesting a historical connection with Sabbatianism. The evidence consists of encounters between Sabbatians and figures of the Jewish enlightenment. One cannot point to encounters between the founding personalities and leaders of the Jewish enlightenment and Sabbatians or Frankists. It is certainly impossible to find any influence of ideas and spiritual sentiments. That is to say, we are dealing at most with entirely incidental, interpersonal encounters. And as for the supposed connection between Zionism and Sabbatianism, this allegation is, to begin with, nothing more than a "*midrash*ic" interpretation based on parallels between the two movements.

Indeed, it is altogether doubtful that we should assess the question of the connection between Sabbatianism and other movements in Judaism by examining this type of data. For while we may be able to discover clear evidence of close encounters between Hassids and Sabbatians or between figures of the enlightenment and Sabbatians, and while we may even discover many Hassids or adherents of the enlightenment who themselves were erstwhile Sabbatians or Frankists, such findings still would not constitute proof that Hassidism, as a wide popular movement, or the Jewish enlightenment, as a movement of the spiritual elite, generated their spiritual content or their social reference-group from Sabbatianism or Frankism. Here, relevant tests should include a determination of the cultural and sociological characteristics of the social group responding to these movements, as well as a substantive examination of the worldviews under consideration. Personal links merely indicate that other movements existed contemporaneously with Sabbatianism. This plurality of movements suggests that Sabbatianism was one manifestation of the crisis of modernity syndrome.

The crisis embodied in Sabbatianism and Frankism must surely have stimulated concerned soul-searching among the Jewish people's attentive and sensitive members. But when we examine Sabbatianism — Sabbatianism as it finally crystallized after the conversion of Sabbatai Sevi — we cannot avoid seeing it as a response to historical reality that originated in misunderstanding and ended in total collapse. Those who were caught up in Sabbatianism found themselves at an impasse.[111] Sabbatianism was, therefore, from both personal and public perspectives, destructive and pathological. The movement was either generated by spiritual illness or it led its adherents to spiritual illness. One could reasonably assume that persons who had become involved in Sabbatianism would subsequently continue attempting to "find their way." It is also reasonable to assume that some of these persons would succeed in overcoming the pathological situation in which they were trapped by finding their way to a positive spiritual movement.

The historically decisive fact emerges from the contrast between (a) Sabbatianism and its transformations, as against (b) Hassidism and the Jewish enlightenment. This contrast highlights all the differences that distinguish (a) a destructive movement catering to strong spiritual impulses but not responding adequately to actual reality, from (b) popular movements that respond adequately to the existing conditions of immanent reality. Clearly, a negative movement can pose the challenge leading to the further development of a distinct positive movement. But by no means is it possible for a negative movement to serve as the base for a positive movement. In order to progress from Sabbatianism and Frankism to Hassidism or to the Jewish enlightenment, Jewish thinkers needed to break loose from the grip of Sabbatianism. That is to

111 Similar claims, albeit rather hyperbolic ones, were made by Baruch Kurzweil in his critical essay "Notes on Gershom Scholem's Sabbatai Sevi," in the book *Ba-Maavak Al Arakhei Ha-Yahadut* (Jerusalem and Tel-Aviv: 1970). As noted above, in the seventh chapter of his book, Scholem assesses Sabbatianism as a destructive movement that reached an impasse. But nevertheless, Scholem attributed quite a decisive role to Sabbatianism in the history of the Jewish people and its modern thought!

138

say, they had to start anew. For this purpose it was necessary to seek healthy sources of sustenance beyond those of the pathological movement. Indeed, this is exemplified by Hassidism and the Jewish enlightenment. Both of these movements reconfronted the social and cultural-religious reality of the Jewish people. In this respect, Hassidism and the Jewish enlightenment constitute the beginnings of unprecedented movements. Moreover, both movements, seeking to anchor themselves in the past, found their moorings in pre-Sabbatian sources. Hassidism anchored it self in the kabbalistic tradition of the *Zohar* and in Lurianic *Kabbalah*, as well as in the thought of the R. Loewe of Prague. The Jewish enlightenment anchored itself in the rationalistic literature and classical philosophy of the early middle ages. Both of these movements adopted a certain stance toward Sabbatianism. This stance cannot be misinterpreted. For both movements, Sabbatianism was the most dangerous contemporaneous phenomenon threatening the people of Israel from within. It might also be said that both these movements recoil from efforts to implement the mystical "option" as a real historical force that actually alters the Jewish people's situation in the "here and now."

There is no dialectical perspective that enables one to trace a positive connection between Sabbatianism and Frankism on the one hand, and Hassidism or the Jewish enlightenment on the other. The reason is actually simple and apparent to any observer: the dialetic of "virtue achieved through sin," or of "redemption accomplished through destruction," allows at most for a short period of several years during which an active national existence is maintained. That is, this dialectic allows only for the short period of time needed to complete the labor of destruction, or to discard all the baggage of negative energy through destructive behavior. Nevertheless, since nothing new is created through this destruction, a movement such as Sabbatianism can anticipate no denouement other than its own end as a movement. Individuals may escape this awful end by abandoning ship while there is still time. Naturally, those who manage to abandon ship will not turn back.

Rather, they will seek out a new spiritual movement. This point has tremendous significance for our study. It embodies one of the important latent motives underlying several characteristics of the *Wissenschaft des Judentums* movement, which Scholem attacked with unjustified vehemence. The Sabbatian and Frankist warning signal was among the main factors for the aversion toward mysticism exhibited by the adherents of Jewish enlightenment and the founders of *Wissenschaft des Judentums*. We will return to this issue later on in the concluding sections of this volume.

ii. Modern Religious Awakening

Scholem supposed that mysticism was destined to play a role in overcoming the crisis generated by Judaism's entrance into modernity. This belief is entirely a matter of prophetic prediction. Even Scholem conceded that his comments here are, in essence, an expression of faith. But this faith is anchored in his overall view of mysticism's place in the Jewish religion.

Scholem's few essays concerning the contemporary spiritual life of Israel's people indicate that he was very concerned as to whether there is a chance for the renewal of a mystical movement within a Judaism that is caught at the highest point of secularization. The portrait of reality that Scholem had observed since the commencement of his scholarly journey was not very promising.

Hassidism was the largest and most salient remnant of a Jewish movement that still drew sustenance from mysticism. But nevertheless, Hassidism seemed to be in the process of deterioration. It contained few new creative expressions. It lacked entirely a deep confrontation with the problem of religion in the context of modernity.

Further, in non-Hassidic Orthodoxy, there was an aversion toward mysticism and toward theological thinking in general. Non-Hassidic Orthodoxy tends to emphasize Toraitic learning in the style of the Lithuanian Jewish academies (*yeshivot*) during the early part of this century. The small dose of religious philosophy that penetrated this toraitic pedagogy was merely an echo of the Lithuanian moralistic (*musar*) movement. Within the religious Judaism that is called "orthodox," one can point to only one creative mystical personality who gained significant influence. Moreover, the mainstream of his thought also manifests a serious confrontation with the reality of modernity. This personality is Isaac Kook. But Kook's thought was crystallized during the early wave of Zionism's development, before the establishment of the Jewish state and prior to the second world war and the holocaust. There has been no creative continuation of his thought. His influence has also become dogmatically rigid and has been intertwined with a process of radicalization. This process has led toward the withdrawal of religion from the fullness of contemporary cultural life.

Indeed, orthodoxy has undergone a process of radicalization leading toward fundamentalism in religious belief and an increased severity in the maintenance of ritualistic ordinances separating the strictly orthodox Jew from the rest of the Jewish people. This process is the most salient phenomenon characterizing orthodoxy among the Jewish people in general, and in the state of Israel in particular.

At least for now, this entails the prevalence of a viewpoint that upholds the distinctly halakhic-institutional attitude as the only means to save "the remnant of Israel" from the monster "secularization." It follows that there is no chance for a revolutionary, daring, and truly responsive mystical awakening from within orthodoxy.[112]

What is the position of non-orthodox religious movements vis-a-vis these issues? An examination of writings by several profound thinkers in these movements may uncover romantic and nostalgic mystical motifs. But inasmuch as such writings represent efforts to confront the present's problems — efforts of this kind, some of them quite deep, can be found in several non-orthodox Jewish thinkers — there is no move toward mysticism. Indeed, the con-

112 Cf. "Reflections on the Possibility of Jewish Mysticism in Our Day."

trary is the case. One still clearly discerns these thinkers' aversion to mysticism coupled with their view that mysticism is a fundamentally negative solution to religious crisis. For this reason, it is not surprising that Scholem concluded his examination of compositions by his generation's theologians with a sense of disappointment that ultimately manifested itself in disparagement. Those deep dimensions which he loved could not be found in his generation's writings. He thus regarded his contemporary theologians as simply inauthentic.[113] But despite all these disappointments, he did not reach despair. Furthermore, he did not change his overall historical-philosophical outlook. In the emptiness, or the inauthenticity of contemporary religious Jewish thought, Scholem saw an affirmation of his own assertion that a generation caught in the midst of crisis is unable to recognize its own depths. This generation is consequently unable to offer the appropriate religious solution. One must first clarify all the implications of the permutations that the Jews underwent through secularization. Only after these processes are spelled out will there be an eruption of the fountain which springs from the closed depths of internal religious experience.

One should not reply to words of prophecy that are anchored in faith. And indeed, is there any basis for a counter-argument to Scholem's position on this issue? It is entirely possible that while these very lines are being written, some thinker is composing a great mystical creation which confronts the spiritual reality of our times and which may generate a movement. But the issue that should concern Jewish thinkers of our time is not whether the awakening of a mystical movement is possible in the future. Rather, Jewish thinkers should be considering how, while preserving historical continuity, the Jewish religion can sustain the authority it needs to unify the Jewish people and to exert a significant influence upon an overall culture that can express its life as a people. Is there any chance that the Jewish religion can continue to exist and to exert influence as a popular religion both in its range of

113 Cf. "Reflections on Jewish Theology."

application and its ability to furnish a comprehensive conceptual guide for those on all spiritual levels? Is it a mystical awakening that will return the Jewish religion to this status?

Questions of this kind can only be answered through lessons drawn from history. But our historical inquiry should include not only the distant past, but also the recent past. One can indeed say that the process of secularization marks a crisis "between" two periods in the history of the people of Israel. But one cannot overlook the fact that this crisis has a considerable history spanning over two hundred years. This constitutes an entire era with its own internal sequence. No Jewish movement which seeks to confront and to renew can overlook the forms of Jewish existence generated during this period. Nor can it ignore the lessons implied by these forms of Jewish existence. Even if a movement criticizes previous forms of experience and thought, it must nonetheless link itself to them and draw sustenance from them.

This will be understood by anyone who credits Scholem's analogy between our period and the time elapsed from the Spanish expulsion to the creation of Lurianic *Kabbalah*. Scholem notes that there is a striking difference between the original and deep creations of mysticism in Safed during the sixteenth century and the rather unoriginal creations produced after the Spanish expulsion. Nevertheless, the creations from Safed represent the culmination of a spiritual enterprise generated throughout the course of generations. The spread of the *Zohar's* influence among the people and the popular dissemination of various Kabbalistic essays written after the Spanish expulsion served as a preparation for later developments. This process embodied specific traces of the subsequent developments in Safedian *Kabbalah*. Similarly, it is inconceivable that in the modern age, the spiritual-religious creation of the future will fail to base itself on existing creations which have been produced during the last few generations.

By observing the history of Judaism, we concluded that even during periods in which there were large and influential mystical movements among the people of Israel, these movements did not sustain the Jewish religion's unity or its continuity from one generation to the next. Rather, this unity and continuity were embodied in the *halakhah*, which is based upon the historical myth of the exodus from Egypt, the revelation of *Torah*, and the vision of future redemption following all the destructions and exiles. Through an examination of the Jewish people's spiritual-religious creations in recent generations, one draws the very same lesson. Indeed, the crisis endured by the Jews in recent generations severely damaged the infrastructure of the historical myth and the *halakhah*. This damage was brought about by scientific research, which displaced traditional learning. It was also brought about by the relativist and secularist consciousness of modernity and by the horrifying experience endured by the Jews during these generations. At no other time was there such an intense and deep feeling that the people of Israel had been abandoned to its destiny.

But nevertheless, those segments of the Jewish people who retained a faith in their unique heritage actually held on, in various ways, either to the complete historical myth and to the *halakhah* in its entirety, or at least to fragments of the myth and to parts of the *halakhah*. Among those who chose the latter option, some held onto fragments of the myth and the *halakhah* in an effort to reattach the myth to its historical roots. They studied history scientifically in an effort to facilitate the continuity of a Jewish culture anchored in history and the tradition it transmits. The careful observer will find that any religious or cultural-national thought which seriously confronts the problem of Jewish culture's continuity, whether through Judaism's religion or its personal-social ethos, does not need to rely upon a mystical foundation. Rather, such thinking needs to appeal to the social-historical elements surrounding the idea of the covenant. Moreover, it was through philosophy's system of thought that creative modern thinkers attempted to confront the values of the tradition in order to continue it within a contemporary conceptual framework.

144

iii. Modern Judaic Scholarship and Theology

Scholem's attitude toward modern Jewish philosophy is related to the criticism he directed at modern Judaic scholarship up to his day.[114] This connection is not surprising. There is a reciprocal influence between the sciences of Judaism and modern Jewish religious thought. This influence is anchored in the essence of these two modes of research and thought. It was the philosophy of Judaism which galvanized the methodological premises of the scientific study of Judaism. And it was scholarly research that validated and confirmed the historically Jewish identity of religious Jewish philosophy. Even when he set out to mount a severe critique of *Wissenschaft des Judentums,* Scholem did so only in light of a particular perspective on Judaism. This is indicated by the fact that he focuses his critique upon *Wissenschaft des Judentums'* attitude toward Jewish mysticism in general, and to the *Kabbalah* in particular.

Scholem thought that this attitude in *Wissenschaft des Judentums* was surely not caused by ignorance. Rather, it was the result of a "prejudice" that dismissed mysticism as an alien element, or even as a phenomenon of distorted spirituality. Scholem attributes this "prejudice" against mysticism to the rationalistic philosophical tendency which he regarded as a characteristic of *Wissenschaft des Judentums.* He explains this particular tendency by reference to the assimilationist-apologetic motivation upon which *Wissenschaft des Judentums* was founded. According to this description, *Wissenschaft des Judentums* was created solely in order to serve the interest of assimilation by qualifying Judaism to join the contemporary European enlightenment. Through their particular description of Judaism, the founders of *Wissenschaft des Judentums* sought to refute the accusations levelled against the Jews, and to bestow a prestigious status upon Judaism. But of course, if this is one's sole purpose, it is no longer necessary to regenerate a Jewish creativity with distinctive characteristics. Mysticism threatens to foil this

114 Cf. "Reflections on *Wissenschaft des Judentums.*"

entire project through its lack of reason and its irrational and particularistic myth. As Scholem portrays it, *Wissenschaft des Judentums* had to ignore mysticism in order to achieve the goal which the founders of scientific study in Judaism set out to accomplish — to give Jewish culture a decent burial in the archives of history.

Scholem's sharp critique coincides with those of several notable Zionist writers and thinkers. It corresponds especially to criticisms by *Ahad Ha'am* and H.N. Bialik against *Wissenschaft des Judentums*.[115] But to these thinkers, *Wissenschaft des Judentums'* neglect of mysticism did not represent the main focus for criticism. Rather, they concentrated on its use of a foreign language and on the way it ensconsed itself in academic philological research. They argued that such actions were not compatible with an overall effort to rejuvenate Hebrew culture by transmitting the Jewish tradition from one generation to the next. Scholem, on the other hand, did not object to the academic character of scientific study in Judaism, nor did he see this as an obstacle to such work for future generations. But he was a partner to the main objection that *Wissenschaft des Judentums* was less interested in rejuvenating Jewish culture than in fitting into the Europeans' scientific academic enterprise.

There is no doubt that there was a kernel of truth in this critique. *Wissenschaft des Judentums* had apologetic motivations and it did indeed attempt to prepare the ground for the integration of the Jews with other peoples. But nevertheless, this critique, especially in Scholem's version, constituted a simplistic generalization and an exaggeration which distorted truth. For, notwithstanding these criticisms, *Wissenschaft des Judentums* upheld the value of studying *Torah* for its own sake. It also sought to sustain the study of *Torah* in a new reality and in accord with new forms of creativity. And even if we ignore all this, there is no basis whatsoever for the claim that, through an abundance of dry rationality

---

115 Ahad Ha-Am, "Al Devar Otsar Ha-Yahadut," in *Kol Kitvei Ahad-Ha-Am*, H.Y. Roth ed. (Tel-Aviv: 1946); H.N. Bialik, "On *Wissenschaft des Judentums*" in Bialik's *Collected Works*.

or a quest for assimilation, *Wissenschaft des Judentums* either treated mysticism negatively or neglected it.

First of all, we must establish that most nineteenth-century scholars of *Wissenschaft des Judentums* believed that they were preparing material and content for a new Jewish creation whether in the context of a national culture (Krochmal and Graetz), in a popular religious culture (Frankel and Luzzatto), or in a distinctively religious framework (Zunz and Geiger). A review of programmatic essays by these authors provides explicit evidence[116] that they strove for a new Jewish creation. Moreover, there was quite a reasonable measure of correlation between their programs and their practice. Under these circumstances, it is unjust to claim that these figures, who devoted the best of their talents and strengths to their respective enterprises, intended only to prepare a "decent burial for Judaism." It is true that this unfortunate phrase was uttered by Steinschneider. But we may regard his utterance as a cynical expression of an old man's pessimism — his sense that wisdom will perish with his death. Indeed, I doubt if we even should see this expression as more than one component of an ambivalent attitude. But whatever the case, most Judaic scholars in the *Wissenschaft des Judentums* movement sought and anticipated a continuation of their work.

One must also systematically examine Scholem's claim that all of *Wissenschaft des Judentums* was founded upon a rationalistic understanding of Judaism. What is the basis for this claim? Apparently, it is the affinity between *Wissenschaft des Judentums* and nineteenth-century Jewish theology that was created in the spirit of Kantian and post-Kantian idealism. Indeed, it is generally correct to assert that Jewish theology of the nineteenth century was created in the spirit of the "religion of reason." It is also generally correct to point to an affinity between this theology and *Wissenschaft des Judentums*. But from Scholem himself, we learn that one must consider those particulars that qualify generalizations. Even

116 See the programmatic essays of Zunz and Wolff in the collection edited by Paul Mendes-Flohr, *Hokhmat Yisrael* (Jerusalem: Merkaz Zalman Shazar, 1980).

147

nineteenth-century Jewish theology is not woven from a single fabric, nor does it manifest a unitary approach to idealistic philosophy. In the case of *Wissenschaft des Judentums*, this qualification should be amplified. Many of its founders were not at all inclined toward philosophy. We find in nineteenth-century Jewish theology a fundamental objection to idealism, especially in its extreme Hegelian form. One also finds a turn toward the historical particularism of Judaism and the perception of a personalistic God.[117] There is, moreover, this paradox: in theology that is permeated with Hegelian idealism, we find a positive attitude toward the dialectical neo-platonic elements of the *Kabbalah*,[118] while in *Wissenschaft des Judentums*, we find many expressions that are not amenable to philosophy and, instead, emphasize religion's experiential contents.[119]

Under these circumstances, our next question seems truly worth examining in a substantive fashion: what trends of Jewish religious thought figured most prominently in these theologians' and scholars' efforts to substantiate their perception of Judaism? If Scholem's critical writings on this point are correct, we would expect to find that these men associate themselves mainly with the philosophy of Maimonides and his students. But as it turns out, we find that most of them are substantively linked with biblical sources and with writings by early rabbinic sages. Their substantive link is facilitated through the religious thought of Bahey Ibn Pekudah, the author of *Hovot Halevavot,* and Judah Halevi, the author of the *Kuzari*. It is Judah Halevi who actually provides a model of Jewish religious consciousness for scholars and thinkers such as Rappoport, Luzzatto, Geiger, Frankel, and Graetz. At the same time, Maimonides' approach attracts criticism from these thinkers. Indeed, some of them severely criticize the Maimonidean

117 The most notable representatives of this approach are Steinheim, Hirsch, and Luzzatto.
118 The most notable representatives of this approach are R. Nahman Krochmal and Samuel Hirsch.
119 This is especially apparent in the work of Abraham Geiger, whose approach is very close to that of Luzzatto, despite their belonging to two opposing religious trends in their day.

approach.[120] Is an affinity with Judah Halevi truly indicative of rationalistic religion? The contrary is the case. The fact is, this positive relation to Judah Halevi coincides with the rejection of Maimonides on the one hand, and mysticism on the other. Consequently, we must find a different and deeper explanation for the scholars' negative attitude toward mysticism. Further, this explanation must not merely refer to simplistic rationalism or to apologetics.

First of all, we must critically assess the implication, suggested in Scholem's writings, that these thinkers ignore or neglect mysticism. Scholars such as Krochmal, Zunz, Graetz and Geiger were well aware of Kabbalistic literature's scope. They also knew how greatly this literature influenced Jewish thought in recent generations. These scholars did not need to discover this through research. Their awareness of the influence of *Kabbalah* resulted from their own direct social experience. After all, *Kabbalah* was very much accepted in pious circles in Galicia and Germany. Indeed, it may be said that precisely for this reason, the founders of the Jewish enlightenment were equipped with a very negative attitude toward *Kabbalah* and mysticism. In moving toward the Jewish enlightenment, they were rebelling first of all against mysticism and *Kabbalah*. (The route of Solomon Maimon from pious Judaism to German philosophy is especially noteworthy here.) These scholars and thinkers recognized that *Kabbalah* dominated the Jews' thoughts, emotions, and modes of response to reality. They regarded the reign of *Kabbalah* as a major obstacle which must be overcome so the people might be saved from deterioration. Could a scholar such as Scholem expect these thinkers to believe otherwise? Could Scholem himself have thought otherwise if he had stood in their place?

In order to relocate these matters in their proper context we must recall, once again, the cases of Sabbatianism and Frankism.

120 The most severe critic of Maimonides was, of course, Luzzatto. Hirsch had a similar stance, but one finds reservations concerning Maimonides among thinkers belonging to the reform movement such as Geiger, and even in the writings of Graetz.

These mystical movements' destructive consequences were still sufficiently tangible to justify an aversion to their ancestral mother, *Kabbalah*. In the nineteenth century they were still vibrant and their impression was still very real. Consequently, we need not refer to dry philosophical rationalism in order to surmise why Judaic scholars and figures of the Jewish enlightenment regarded *Kabbalah* negatively. *Kabbalah* was seen as the source of a spiritual illness which distorts man's orientation and his ability to formulate a relevant response to actual reality, thereby resulting in the demise of those caught in its web. Those seeking to lead the Jewish people toward a true confrontation with its problems needed to guide it back to spiritual sanity. It is difficult to blame persons living in that reality for seeing matters from their manifest side and for failing to reach a fuller recognition of the light buried in the depths. From their perspective, they could see matters only as they did.

However, it is true that beyond the historical confrontation with Sabbatianism and Frankism there was an essential difference of spiritual disposition between the mystical attitude and the attitude exhibited by adherents of Jewish enlightenment and scholars involved in *Wissenschaft des Judentums*. This difference truly characterizes the contrast between pious Judaism's spiritual orientation and that of secular modern western culture. At issue is not rationalism, but a basic activist stance. The activist approach turns outward from its position of interiority. Its purpose is to shape the world in accord with human ideals.

The activist disposition thus seeks to exhaust thought, feeling and will in an effort to elevate man's condition. It seeks to achieve its end by shaping man's natural and social environment. This outward disposition was diametrically opposed to the personality's spiritual disposition. The mystic turns inward, away from the world. He further directs his active energy to interiority. Indeed, he actually deals passively with the earthly environment of nature and society, for he assumes that activity in the higher spheres affects earthly reality.

Even in his religion, the modern Jew strives to attain an activist stance toward the world. A careful examination reveals that this basic orientation actually led thinkers of the post-enlightenment period to treat mysticism as a negative moral-religious phenomenon. This applies to thinkers who, even in Scholem's opinion, had already distanced themselves from simplistic rationalistic idealism and had drawn closer to the experiential mystical dimension of religion. The list of these thinkers includes S.R. Hirsch, Hermann Cohen (in his final work), Franz Rosenzweig, and Martin Buber. One may also add the original thought of A.D. Gordon to this list. The focus of their objection to mysticism was the mystic's passive attitude to the earthly "here and now" as realms of man's responsibility. As they saw it, man indeed must shape reality directly in the spirit of faith, but his means should be action. For this reason, man must know the world as it is, through the tools of scientific research. In the eyes of these thinkers, who stand far from simplistic rationalism, herein lies the original attitude of biblical piety. Furthermore, they believe that this attitude is diametrically opposed to the mystical disposition.

Between the pedagogical discipline of Kabbalistic *midrash* and the academic discipline of the Jewish enlightenment lay a further contradiction. The Jewish enlightenment adhered to critical, historical-philological, and scientific research. This type of distinction carries decisive weight, for the philological-historical discipline posited by *Wissenschaft des Judentums'* founders as a base to their enterprise could not easily coexist with the academic discipline of traditional learning, especially as this tradition was crystallized in Eastern and Central Europe. It could not be compatible with *halakhah*'s hair-splitting argumentation or with the Kabbalistic literature's far-reaching midrashic mode of exegesis. The essential point at issue here is not rationalism, but rather the correct way to uncover truth in the sources. In such a controversy, there is no room for compromise.

The scholar who has been convinced that the critical-historical, scientific method is valid will dismiss the midrashic approach,

151

especially in its kabbalistic transformations, as a distortion and a corruption. Such a person will simply demand to be rid of the rejected method.

Significantly, as long as the controversy was raging over the validity of alternative methods for comprehending and interpreting the sources, scholars could not show any willingness for compromise. Only when the scientific method becomes established and institutionalized and attains public recognition can it be used for studying the literature of Talmudic argumentation and of *midrash*. The scholar studying this literature may then seek to understand its principles and to penetrate its content empathetically. In this way, he may even reach a level of over-enthusiasm and love. To his surprise, he may discover that this literature embodies great truths and real insightfulness. But even these treasures are discovered by the scholar only through his own method of textual research and interpretation. In his study of talmudic argumentation and *midrash*, he also remains a modern philologist and historian. Indeed, for the first founders of the Jewish enlightenment and *Wissenschaft des Judentums*, the time was not yet ripe for the philological study of anti-philological exegetical literature. They were struggling to establish the legitimacy of their ways and to impose their methods upon Jewish education. It is possible that this primary motivation was accompanied by external apologetic considerations. So what was seen as a distortion certainly was not something to be proudly displayed before others. But basically, we are dealing here with a substantive controversy over the legitimacy of the new *Wissenschaft des Judentums'* scholarly approach.

Ultimately *Wissenschaft des Judentums* became established as a discipline. It developed into one that was well known to the public, one that achieved respectable results. Only at that point was a path opened for studying the Jewish literature that had shaped the traditional approach to Jewish learning. This literature could now be examined in accord with the same disciplinary tools employed by *Wissenschaft des Judentums*. In this context, it is no exaggeration to say that Gershom Scholem's turn to the study of Jewish mysticism and *Kabbalah* precisely represented a major conquest for *Wissenschaft des Judentums*. The historical-philological discipline had overcome the academic disciplines of traditional exegesis and *Kabbalah*. For alas, it was through Scholem's own hands that *Kabbalah* was first taken over by philological and historical research. Thus, it would seem reasonable to demand from him the degree of historical reflection needed to determine one simple point.

Scholem's own scholarly work on *Kabbalah* was a direct continuation of *Wissenschaft des Judentums* insofar as it applied the same disciplines which that movement had struggled to inculcate. He directly based himself upon the achievements of *Wissenschaft des Judentums*. Without the disciplines of *Wissenschaft des Judentums*, his scholarly enterprise would have been entirely impossible. Moreover, despite his remarkable empathetic identification with Jewish mysticism as an object of research, Scholem's methodological discipline expresses the unbridgeable gap between himself and the sources that he studied. He adhered to this discipline no less fanatically than Steinschneider or Graetz, the objects of his moral wrath. No matter how enthusiastically he responded to the sources, or how strongly he felt the roots of his soul were anchored in mysticism, in his scholarly writings Scholem is not a Kabbalist. Rather, he is a scholar, a philologist, and a historian. His methods represent that same "rationalism" for which he denounces his predecessors in the *Wissenschaft des Judentums*. This is why there is no substantive link between his research and the objects of his research. He does not set out to interpret his sources in order to show how they can be upheld by persons such as himself. Rather, his sole intention — and his sole accomplishment — consisted in showing how and under what circumstances the Kabbalists could uphold their beliefs.

At this juncture, it is worth remembering that Scholem's predecessors had a different attitude toward the sources that they saw as expressions of authentic Judaism. They saw themselves as scholars and as critical men of science. But Scholem's predecessors studied Scripture, *halakhah*, aggadic works by early rabbinic sages, liturgical works and ethical literature in order to uncover themes that could be meaningful for themselves and for their contemporaries, whether they be believing Jews or simply persons wishing to sustain Judaism as a culture. They were indeed aware of the differences between their way of thinking and studying and the way of thought and study embodied in the sources. But through philological-historical reflection, they acquired the tools needed to extract from the aforementioned sources (but not from the *Kabbalah*!) themes that they thought could serve as the source for a new Jewish creation. It follows that their longing for spiritual kinship with the sources directly influenced their negative attitude to *Kabbalah*. By contrast, Scholem's positive attitude to *Kabbalah* clearly involves relinquishing such a connection. It was Scholem himself who defined his enterprise exclusively within the realm of scholarship!

Thus, Scholem manifests a considerable measure of unbefitting ingratitude in his excessive critique of modern Judaic scholarship's enterprise up to his day. He did not properly appreciate its contribution, and he did not properly recognize his indebtedness to its accomplishments. But it seems that over and above the issue of redressing this historical injustice, there remain for us other questions of substantive import. For instance, from whence could modern Jewish thought derive its themes? To what could modern Jewish thought adhere in order to generate a creation that represented continuity with the past and yet was also capable of confronting modern culture's challenges? These questions lead us to our concluding discussion of Scholem's views on Jewish theology in the nineteenth and twentieth centuries.

There was a connection between Scholem's attitude toward *Wissenschaft des Judentums* and his attitude toward modern Jewish theology and philosophy. This link finds expression in Scholem's judging them both by an identical criterion, their attitude toward mysticism and *Kabbalah*. He refuses to forgive liberal theologians such as Formstecher, Abraham Geiger, Kaufman Kohler, Moritz Lazaruss and Hermann Cohen, or neo-orthodox theologians such as S.R. Hirsch for their sin of manifesting a negative attitude toward *Kabbalah*. In Scholem's opinion, *Kabbalah* functioned as the central spiritual force of Judaism, especially during the transition from the middle ages to modernity. He further believed that the neglect of *Kabbalah* prevented orthodoxy from retaining anything more than the institutionalized and fossilized shell of fundamental dogma and *halakhah*. Moreover, liberal Judaism retained nothing more than rationalistic dogmatics and sentimentalist moralism as a substitute for real religion. Even neo-orthodoxy did not achieve much more than halakhic rigidity accompanied by apologetic hermeneutics. A vital religious content still existed in Hassidic movements that adhered to mysticism, but this vital religious consciousness did not remain in orthodoxy, and certainly not in the movements that opposed orthodoxy.

Scholem's early critique is simple and decisive. Its operative criterion is to the fore. In Scholem's later essays his critique becomes more complicated. There, his position evolves into a convoluted web of arguments. Although these arguments were formulated in sharp and uncompromising language, they were not thoroughly substantiated or clarified. Two methodological distinctions stand out from this web of arguments. But rather than defining and substantiating these distinctions, Scholem repeatedly mixes them together. He thereby creates a polemical "mist of battle" that facilitates a surprise attack from every direction.

The first contrast concerns the shift in the orientation of Jewish theology from the late nineteenth century to the early twentieth century.

The second contrast involves the aforementioned differences between (a) Kabbalistic mysticism, with its characteristic myth, and (b) the prophetic-historical myth that was sustained in writings by early rabbinic and medieval sages.

Jewish theology in the nineteenth century was created mostly in Germany, or at least under the influence of German idealism. For

155

the most part, this theology truly inclined toward reducing Judaism to a moral way of life guided by reason. In most of its
expressions, it tended to de-mythologize Judaism or to enable
history to engulf the historical myth.[121] On the other hand, beginning with Hermann Cohen's *Religion of Reason from the Sources of
Judaism*, twentieth-century theology turned in an existentialist
direction that stresses the presence of God and man in creation,
revelation and redemption. This change took on an intense and
inspirational character in Franz Rosenzweig's *The Star of Redemption*. Initially, Scholem's evaluation of the book was very enthusiastic.[122] He sensed a mystical depth in Rosenzweig's experiential
view of religion, even though Rosenzweig himself justifiably saw
these matters in a different light. But it is interesting to note that
Scholem's enthusiasm for *The Star of Redemption* declined over the
years. In his later essays, one finds an erosion of all distinctions
between Jewish theologians of the nineteenth century and their
counterparts in the twentieth. They all fall within Scholem's category of "modern," and their contribution is uniformly dismissed
with disappointment. In Scholem's opinion, even theologians who
wrote in the spirit of existentialism did not manage to overcome
the lack of authenticity inherent in religious thought that takes
account of scientific discipline. Further, the existentially-oriented
theologians stand far from the primal, mythical experience of
revelation. So even they lack authority. They also lack the ability
to lead the Jews by expounding a teaching that shapes a way of
life.[123]

What is the root of this failure? If we seek an answer in
Scholem's writings, we must delineate his second contrast mentioned above. In Scholem's opinion, modern Jewish theology's
main weakness is its inability to sustain the tenet of "*Torah* from
Heaven" in its fundamental sense. Only by maintaining this tenet
in its plain sense, without too many sophisticated subtleties, can

---

121 There were, as we said, exceptions to this rule. We will return to these later on.
122 See the essay on Franz Rosenzweig and his book *The Star of Redemption* in *Explications and Implications*, pp. 407-25.
123 See "Reflections on Jewish Theology."

the Jewish community be guided toward a life governed by *Torah* and divine commandments. Yet the basic elements of the modern theological worldview do not uphold the tenet. For this reason, any theology which recognizes scientific biblical criticism and allows the historical study of Oral *Torah* must fail.

As a matter of course, this point also explains the success of the one religious movement that remained faithful to the tenet of "*Torah* from heaven" in its fundamental sense, namely, the movement called "orthodoxy." And not surprisingly, Scholem's relation to orthodoxy is a prime example of ambivalence in feeling and thought. He reserves some harsh words of criticism for Orthodoxy. In contrast to mysticism's religious daring, it is indeed fossilized and lacking in depth and vitality. Yet when Scholem compares orthodoxy to the other modern religious movements he must concede its advantage. Indeed, a distinct tone of envy emanates from his writings on it. As a person educated in secular western humanistic culture, Scholem himself could neither accept orthodox fundamentalism nor embrace orthodox pedagogy, which insists on ignoring philology and history. He himself was unwilling to accept the obligation to obey the religious commandments, and he rejected orthodoxy's effort to impose these commandments upon the secular Jewish public. But he admitted that if authentic Jewish religion is still sustained in any sense among the Jewish people, then it is orthodoxy that prevents this flame from being extinguished.

Is there mysticism in orthodoxy? Not necessarily. Insofar as we refer to the orthodox movement that was galvanized after the period of Jewish emancipation, we are dealing with a trend of fundamentalism that is unwilling to risk either philosophy or mysticism. Does this mean that, after all, one must distinguish (a) mysticism and its myth from (b) the historical myth of the exodus from Egypt and the revelation of *Torah*? Is the latter needed to sustain the Jew's fundamental belief in "*Torah* from heaven"? This distinction between "mystical myth" and "historical myth" logically follows from Scholem's attitude toward orthodoxy. But

157

while Scholem stands on the verge of adopting this distinction at several points, he nevertheless refuses to formulate it.[124] Scholem's coyness here produces the impression that, in his opinion, a belief in the myth of Sinaitic revelation falls within the bounds of mysticism. Orthodoxy, then, has only one deficiency: it holds onto the seed of mysticism while lacking the courage to let it grow and develop. Orthodoxy may indeed be closer to mysticism than any other religious movement in modernity, but, like Franz Rosenzweig's version of existentialism, for its own reasons it steers away from mysticism.[125]

So no contemporary religious movement holds the secret for overcoming the divine hiddenness (*hester panim*) of our time. We can find the solution only after time has brought this great crisis to its full fruition. Then the abyss will open before our eyes. Its contours will be revealed, depth upon depth. A new mystical movement will erupt from the core of the mystical myth. This movement will be as revolutionary as its predecessors — it may even be more revolutionary, for it will have to overcome a crisis seven times more severe than the previous ones. But this movement will be crowned as "the true successor." Until that time, we must wait patiently. We must not rely upon inauthentic solutions, upon illusory substitutes. But what of those who are not protected by a warm, narrow orthodoxy — what shall they do until the hour of revelation arrives? Scholem had only one suggestion, and he personally seemed to find it sufficient. His suggestion was empathetically to study Judaism's sources and especially the sources of mystical thought. Through empathetic study, one forges a connection and possibly prepares in some way for the destined renewal.[126]

At this point, one clearly sees that the lack of distinction between the mystical myth and the historical myth continues to be a fertile source for Scholem's untenable arguments. Now, the

---

124 See especially the aforementioned essay "Three Types of Jewish Piety" in *Explications and Implications*, pp. 541-556.

125 See the essay "Reflections on the Possibility of Jewish Mysticism in Our Day."

126 Scholem expressed these views most elaborately in conversation.

inappropriate assertions concern some thinkers' efforts to confront Judaism's modern crisis. It is surely correct to say that the central issue for contemporary Jewish theology is the belief in *Torah* as an authority dictating a community's way-of-life. Indeed, all the Jewish thinkers of the nineteenth and twentieth centuries explicitly attest to this issue's centrality.[127]

But there is no basis for assuming that a belief in *"Torah* from heaven"* which carries certain duties for the believer must be fundamental in the orthodox sense of that term. Furthermore, there is no basis for assuming that only mysticism makes such a belief possible. Such a necessary link was never posited during any period in Judaism's history and certainly not during the modern era. In fact there has been a retreat from mysticism within orthodoxy, even in the orthodox wing which has refused to compromise with the values of secular culture. Orthodoxy has firmly held to halakhic study of *Torah* and to obedience to the commandments' authority. It has simultaneously neglected philosophical and kabbalistic discussions of the "rationale" underlying the divine ordinances. These developments indicate that there is no necessary link between mysticism and the belief in *"Torah* from heaven."* They further suggest that, under certain circumstances, the belief actually may be endangered by such a link.

The same conclusion is suggested by the neo-orthodoxy founded by S.R. Hirsch. In one of his essays, Scholem claimed that there is a suppressed mystical element in the thought of S.R. Hirsch. But at no point in Hirsch's writings can one find a basis for this claim, except for the obvious fact that he affirms experiential religion. In his extensive writings on the rationale underlying the ordinances, we find no trace of mysticism. All the ordinances are directed toward making loyalty and obedience habitual in man. In addition, the ordinances guide the individual to act in a manner that benefits all other creatures, his fellow men, and himself. These deeds are in harmony with the purpose of God's creation. If

---

127 Cf. Julius Guttman's assertions in the essay "On the Foundations of Judaism" in *Religion and Knowledge* (Jerusalem: Magnes, 1955), p. 259ff.

Hirsch's writings do express an experience of direct presence before God, then it is the experience of the slave who lovingly obeys his master's commands. And if any myth does exist in Hirsch's writings, it is the myth of Genesis and Exodus, including the stories of the creation, the patriarchs, the exodus from Egypt, and the Sinaitic revelation. In the diaspora, the Jews experience the cosmic and historical myth of creation, exile and redemption. Their experience is facilitated by a life that revolves upon the cyclical religious axis of weekly, monthly and yearly time. In this manner, they experience God's providence.

In a somewhat different manner one can point to the vitality of this same myth in the writings of Hermann Cohen and Franz Rosenzweig — even in the work of Martin Buber. If Scholem argues that these thinkers also draw near to mysticism without admitting it, he can refer only to their vital connection with the historical myth. The catch in this argument is that their connection to the myth is explicitly and overtly elaborated in the writings of Cohen, Rosenzweig and Buber, and yet this does not deter these thinkers from treating mysticism negatively and Judah Halevi positively.[128] Does this not suggest the need to re-examine the generalization that any religious expression which sustains the mythical consciousness beyond its initial innocent stage falls within the category of mysticism? All of these thinkers — and it is worth adding J. Heschel to this list — distinguish clearly between the mythical element on the one hand, and mysticism on the other. They all attempted to provide subtle and sensitive phenomenological descriptions of the biblical myth's special character as well as its continuation in the writings of early rabbinic sages. As it turns out, it is precisely such attempts which seem to represent these thinkers' most important contributions. For these descriptions contributed to Judaism's self-understanding. This was essential for the re-orientation required by modernity.

---

128 The leading proponents of this view are Franz Rosenzweig and Martin Buber, but even Hermann Cohen notes that even at the stage of its full rational development, Judaism did not sever its link with the myth. See *The Religion of Reason*, Ch. I, paragraphs 3-11.

That is to say, in order correctly to assess Jewish theology's recent achievements, we must accept the clear distinction between (a) mysticism, and (b) the historical myth of Judaism together with the way of life ordained by it. Most nineteenth-century Jewish theology attempted to resolve the problems of faith by demythologizing Judaism, replacing history's mythical component with lawfulness based on reason. Simultaneously, the theologians translated "authoritative religious injunctions that were revealed through divine fiat" into "moral imperatives of reason." This process truly represents the "retreat" of religious experience. Indeed, it does not seem possible thus to preserve a large community that lives for a significant period of time within the sphere of a discernably full Jewish life.

But already in the nineteenth century, one sees the beginnings of a different theology that strives for a deeper understanding of the Jewish religious myth.

We are not only referring to S.R. Hirsch and to neo-orthodoxy, which actually succeeded in galvanizing into a movement. We refer also to authentic religious thinkers like Steinheim and Samuel Hirsch. These men blazed a trail which was later cleared and expanded by the most prominent Jewish theologians of the twentieth century. Modern theology has greatly contributed to the formation of the contemporary Jew's religious consciousness. Of course, this contribution is evident in those areas of spiritual, religious and moral education in which theology can be expected to exercise an influence.

First of all, the modern theologians made an important contribution in the intellectual realm. They brought the symbols and ordinances of toraitic Judaism nearer to the conceptual culture that developed in the modern era. They also assisted the learned Jew who wished to identify with his people's tradition and to live according to its patterns. With theology's assistance, this Jew was able to express his worldview in a manner that was valid and persuasive within the context of the debates and exchanges taking place at the apex of his culture's intellectual achievement. In addition, these thinkers helped the learned Jew to define the boundaries of agreement and controversy between the Jewish people's faith and the scale of values in the surrounding secular western culture. Obviously, the learned Jew could now cope better with his environment. That is, he could affirm elements that could be linked with his conceptions, and reject those which contradicted them. Finally, modern theology also provides guidelines for a Jewish way of life in Jewish communities under contemporary social-cultural conditions.

What more can one expect from creations in the realm of theology? Indeed, was there ever any single theology which succeeded in resolving the problems of faith in a way that was satisfactory for all Jews? Was there ever any theology that ensured the believer's personal religious adherence by persuasive solutions on an intellectual plain?

It is certainly possible that contemporary Jewish theologies did not succeed in sustaining the authoritative position of *Torah* for the larger Jewish publics. But this does not imply a deficiency or a lack of authenticity in the religious thought which these theologies express. As we said, by itself, no theology was able to establish the authority needed to shape a complete way of life. Together with the intellectual effort of theologians there must also be a creative effort in the social-institutional realm. Such efforts must strive to regenerate the Jewish community. There must also be creativity in the halakhic realm. That is, Jews must adapt the *halakhah* to contemporary circumstances by dealing with both the applicability of its norms and their transparent religious significance. Theological thought is indeed a vital component in this kind of social and halakhic creation. But in order for intellectual solutions to achieve practical application, one must have specific and distinct social and halakhic tools that operate within their respective disciplines. Why have creative efforts in these areas up to the present day been so sluggish and inadequate? This question calls for a separate deliberation and one which probably should make exhaustive use of the tools of the social sciences. However, we can assert that the cause of this problem does not lie in the absence of authentic theology. Furthermore, we can say that deliverance from this predicament will not be brought about by a more authentic and mythically rooted theology.

iv. Judaism's Contemporary Crisis

The preceding argument requires qualification. Our appreciative comments about contemporary Jewish theology's contributions fall within the category of subjective impressions. There are no exact scientific criteria for evaluating theological teachings' scope of influence, and certainly there are no precise measures of the depth or authenticity of their impact. At most, one can point to certain elite groups that absorbed some particular influence from theology and applied it in an educational enterprise. Anything further represents nothing more than an impression derived from one's personal response. It is clear that if we take as our criteria (a) the scope of elite groups that are influenced, and (b) the degree of their adherence to these influences, then all the theologies of our day cannot even be compared in status with Kabbalistic theology of the sixteenth, seventeenth and eighteenth centuries. This fact surely indicates the extent of our contemporary crisis. The social infrastructure of the Jewish religious way of life has been undermined and almost demolished.

One may conclude that the reason for these declines in intensity and in scope of religious influence lies in the shallowness and lack of authenticity of influential Jewish thought. One may even agree with Scholem that we are necessarily subjected to shallowness today because the depths are still hidden from our view. But it remains doubtful whether we should accept his suggestion. That is, we cannot, as he recommends, either cease our search, sit tight in hopeful silence and anticipate a revelation of the depths, or occupy ourselves with the devoted and empathetic study of theological-mystical sources that do not provoke our questions. The portrait of cosmic, social, political and historical reality

163

depicted in these theological-mystical sources bears no resemblance to that reality which, to the best of our knowledge, stands before our eyes today. In our opinion, a respectable and significant function is reserved for this kind of study. Such studies certainly are required for the regenerative creative process. But can this enterprise by itself provide an assurance of Judaism's continuity? Can it alone offer more than a romantic substitute for authentic religious experience?

Behind these questions lies another problem: there is reason to question the parallel Scholem draws between (a) the span of time that elapsed from the Spanish expulsion to the creation of Lurianic *Kabbalah*, and (b) the time which supposedly must still elapse before we have an appropriate response to the crisis generated by our contemporary encounter with secular culture. At the base of Scholem's argument-by-analogy lies the supposition that after every major historical upheaval there is a significant span of time during which history reverts to a phase of stability resting on new foundations. Is this indeed true in our day as well?

The historical experience of over two hundred years serves to undermine Scholem's affirmative conclusion. He borrows his conclusion from the study of antiquity. In ancient times the process of change seemed slow. Potential for change accumulated over long periods before generating a breach in an existing structure. In our day, the processes of change are much quicker. Moreover, they are immediately discernible in the foundational structures themselves. Western society is changing before our eyes at an ever-increasing pace. Indeed, there is no sign on the horizon of a fixed and stationary social-cultural structure that will furnish the observer with a calm perspective. Paradoxically, it seems a tenable idea that constant change is the only stable element of contemporary secular culture! And it is this feature that characterizes our era as modern.

The Jewish people is located at the center of this process of transformation. The situation of the Jewish people is rapidly changing. By the time we define its situation, we discover that it has changed. Thus, it seems appropriate to conclude that the preservation of continuity throughout such processes of change requires a constant effort which cannot be abandoned for even a moment. If you drop this task for just one day, you will fall two days behind. For this reason, even the most shallow solution seems preferable to a romantic contemplation of the past and future. So, it is not sound advice to rest content with the devoted work of professors who engage in study and scholarship. The enterprise of creative thought, accompanied by creative work in the area of social norms, must be continued. No generation is entitled to excuse itself from whatever small accomplishments it can achieve.

PART 3.

CONCLUSION

Chapter 8

THE VALUE OF SCHOLEM'S SCHOLARLY ENTERPRISE

At the conclusion of our comprehensive discussion, readers should remember that we have been concerned with the "aura" surrounding Scholem's elaborate work on the history of Jewish mysticism, not with the work itself. Scholem provided detailed studies of ancient mysticism, of Spanish *Kabbalah* in general and the *Zohar* in particular, of Safedian *Kabbalah,* and of Sabbatianism and Hassidism. These studies deserve the fundamental esteem of those who continue to explore these mystical sources and to uncover their hidden treasures. Undoubtedly Scholem's work represents a monumental enterprise. It provided some permanently valuable treasures not only for the scientific study of Judaism, but for all progressive thought that depends on solid foundations and deep roots.

We have concerned ourselves only with Scholem's general views and programmatic approaches. We have been interested in (a) how he deciphered the secret of Judaism's unity and continuity, (b) how he explained the crisis that the Jewish religion and people underwent in modern times, and (c) the role he assigned to modern Judaic scholarship and to contemporary Jewish theology.

Our evaluation is called for because of the central role Scholem played in crystallizing programmatic positions regarding the study of Judaism both in Israel and abroad. His views have exercised a tremendous influence. To no small extent, they determined the orientations of research and the evaluation of creative Jewish thought that has been regenerated in modern times. So despite all the respect and gratitude contemporary scholars owe Scholem for his vast enterprise, they must re-examine teachings which often — all too often — were accepted as the firm and indubitable words of an authority who may not be questioned. Re-examination is called for by the scientific discipline of inquiry taught by Scholem himself. In the absence of such re-examination, we are liable to err

169

and to lose our way. We may be misled by hidden prejudices deriving from particular circumstances that affected the development of Scholem's personality and from the cultural environment in which he was raised. For all these reasons, we must re-orient our response to Scholem's ideas. Otherwise, the intense and concentrated light that Scholem cast upon the study of Jewish mysticism throughout the generations will turn into a veil obscuring our vision so that we may no longer see the wide realms that surround and transcend mysticism.

Invocation, 64
Irrational, 145
Islam, 25, 75, 107
Israelite religion, 59, 61-67, 70, 74, 91, 94

Jewish enlightenment, 85, 86, 135-39, 148-51
Jewish law, 5
Job, 68, 74
Jones, R., 24
Judaea, 98, 99
Judah Halevi, 42, 115, 116, 147, 148, 159
Judaic scholarship, 1, 4, 9, 11, 12, 21, 144, 153, 167
Judaica, 9

Kabbalah, 1, 2, 7, 12, 13, 22, 23, 27, 28, 30, 31, 34, 37, 39,
    43, 47, 70, 71, 77-81, 87-89, 101-103, 117, 118, 123,
    126-28, 133, 135, 136, 138, 142-44, 147-49, 151-53,
    162, 167
Kabbalists, 32, 42, 70, 77, 88, 90, 117, 126, 152
Kadushin, 101
Kedushah, 100
Kohler, K., 62, 153
Kook, I., 140
Krochmal, N., 75, 146-48
Kurzweil, B., 11, 85, 137
Kuzari, 42, 115, 116, 147

Lazaruss, M., 153
Lithuanian Jewish academies, 140
Liturgical poets, 127
Liturgy, 32, 33, 44, 94, 97, 99-101
Loewe, 138
Lore, 94, 97
Lower spheres, 44, 131
Luria, I., 37, 136

Magic, 75, 76, 92
Maimon, S., 148